<u>Image of God</u> Series 1

Seeing the Unseen

Educating in the Twilight Zone of God's Glory

But, as this faith, which works by love, begins to penetrate the soul, it tends, through the vital power of goodness, to change into sight, so that the holy and perfect in heart catch glimpses of that ineffable beauty whose full vision is our highest happiness. Here, then, surely, is the answer to your question about the beginning and the end of our endeavor. We begin in faith, we are perfected in sight.

—Augustine of Hippo,
Handbook (Enchiridion), 1:5-7

by Dana Roberts, M.A., M.T.S.

Copyright © 2010 by Dana Roberts, M.A., M.T.S.

Seeing the Unseen
by Dana Roberts, M.A., M.T.S.

Printed in the United States of America

ISBN 9781609572211

All rights reserved solely by the author. The author guarantees all contents are original and do not infringe upon the legal rights of any other person or work. No part of this book may be reproduced in any form without the permission of the author. The views expressed in this book are not necessarily those of the publisher.

Unless otherwise indicated, Bible quotations are taken from The New International Version of the Bible. Copyright © 1973, 1978, 1984 by International Bible Society.

Cover illustration. Detail of *Les disciples Pierre et Jean courant au Sépulcre le matin de la Résurrection* 1898 by Eugene Burnand. Musee d'Orsay, Paris

Front page illustration. By John Constable

www.xulonpress.com

Seeing the Unseen
Educating in the Twilight Zone of God's Glory

Introduction

For our light and momentary troubles are achieving for us an eternal glory that far outweighs them all. So we fix our eyes not on what is **seen**, but on what is **unseen**. For what is **seen** is temporary, but what is **unseen** is eternal. 2 cor 4:17f NIV

2 Corinthians 4:17 and 18 are the verses that inspired this book. How can you possibly "fix your eyes . . . on what is unseen"? I had an inkling of the answer in childhood and as a young Christian. Then the answer was lost. I was just too busy "serving God" to look. With time my eyes refocused. I saw again. I started thinking and searching for an explanation. Why the remission of my near-sightedness? Why can I see again the beauty and the glory?

Though reading can give eyestrain it can also heal. Reading a book lets an author, even from the distant past, speak into the inner ear of the heart. Some authors hide their personality in dry academic dissertations. Others write in political pretentious "I did no wrong" ways. But a good script lets you hear the heart of the author. The best books are personal and confessional. In *Oliver Twist*, Charles Dickens confesses his deep sorrow and compassion for the poor of Victorian London. From her adolescent diary Anne Frank whispers her fears and joys as a

Jew, a teenager and as a living soul. Harpo Marx speaks! And Harpo, the silent partner of the Marx Bothers, spoke very well in his 1962 biography. Others speak of things unseen rarely known by those outside the world of faith. Blaise Pascal, Dallas Willard, C. S. Lewis, John Done, Gospel writers, St. Paul and others also see the unseen. Often you have to read between the lines, observe behavior, and blend their words and your thoughts with great philosophy and science to understand even more. This book is my eye prescription. If it works recommend it to others.

Acknowledgments, outright thanks are called for. Can't say enough about my family, especially my wife Sherry. She patiently let me walk around in a meditative daze as I pondered mysteries beyond my pay grade. My son Andrew went through the manuscript and picked up grammatical errors and obfuscations like an NCIS staffer. And there was Jeff Paul's and Don Redmon's Bible study. The whole class took what they read in Scriptures and search for insights from their own lives to fill the gaps in my own head. Thank you, ladies and gentleman.

Finally a dedication: To the great teachers of this world. I salute such great teacher-writers as Jacques Barzan, Dr. Daniel Robinson of Georgetown University, Emory University Professor Luke Timothy Johnson, art historians William Kloss and Catherine Scallen (I share their love of Northern Renaissance art and the American landscape tradition.), and some great talk show hosts and columnists. Over the years I had many professors. The names that stick in the head as 'the greats' also shared a part of their character as they taught. There were more than dry academics. Honor goes to Doctors Jordan Fiore, T. Christy Wilson, Douglas Stuart, David Scholer and J. Glen Gould. Yet there is so many other teachers we ought to pay honor to. Sometimes a son or daughter, an elementary school teacher, a friend or neighbor taught me something beyond the classroom "the peace that passes all understanding."

This is the first book in the Image of God Series. Book two is the personal practical application of book one. It will explain and illustrate how the meditating heart can serve as an antidote to contemporary culture's infatuation with unrealistic romance, group thinking, violence, and entertainment technology. The third book is about environmentalism. It's focus is not on bird sanctuaries or cleaning China's river. They are important. But this is more about getting back our sense of priority, and rejecting distorted advertising and Hollywood images. It is about the domicile environment we create in our homes, our offices and schools. Ideas and images we passively take in through our senses are reconstructed in the phantom images and feelings of our hearts.

Chapter One

Seeing the Unseen

"So, What's to see?" My eighth-grade Latin teachers asked. He's caught me staring outside and listening to the wind rustling the oak leaves. The 'academically correct' answers are "Nothing" or "Sorry, I wasn't paying attention." But that's not the the truth, the whole truth. I was trying to see something wonderful, what one hymn writer says is "beyond the sunset."

I've been a Christian for nearly fifty years. I can't remember hearing a sermon explaining how to "see the unseen." St Paul's words seem so mysterious. He does tell us that the unseen is "eternal." But, what does that mean? The boy in M. Night Shyamalan's film *Sixth Sense* (1999) sees "dead people . . . all the time." Aren't the souls of the saints eternal? Yet after the ascension of Jesus the dead are not to be seen. Hands are lifted up to Heaven in churches not hands down on tables or Ouija boards awaiting a tap, a rap from a dead relative. The church is in the Spirit but not into spiritualism.

There are persons purporting to see unseen angels and demons. I'd love to see and hear an angel who can sing like Della Reese. Bring on the angel of death. I know my destination. Angels were seen in Biblical days, especially at holy places and holy events. Yet Hebrews 13:2 tells us " Be not forgetful to entertain strangers: for thereby some have entertained angels unawares." The strangers may be angels but even the early church couldn't tell. I met a man who claimed to see demons. Perhaps he did . . . looking in a mirror. He defrauded a number of Christians of their savings.

There are other vision verses that come to mind . . .

> Thy word *is* a lamp unto my feet, and a light unto my path. —Psalm 119:105 KJV

My Bible doesn't glow in the dark.

> In the beginning was the Word, and the Word was with God, and the Word was God. The same was in the beginning with God. All things were made by him; and without him was not any thing made that was made. In him was life; and the life was the light of men. John 1:1-4

> Then spake Jesus again unto them, saying, I am the light of the world: he that followeth me shall not walk in darkness, but shall have the light of life.—John 8:12 (KJV)

> "This is the message we have heard from him and declare to you: God is light; in Him there is no darkness at all."—1 John 1:5

Did Jesus glow in the dark? No. His light was visible just as much in the noon day sun as in the evening.

> Ye are the light of the world. A city that is set on an hill cannot be hid. Neither do men light a candle, and put it under a bushel, but on a candlestick; and it giveth light unto all that are in the house. Let your light so shine before men, that they may see your good works,

> and glorify your Father which is in heaven.—Matthew 5:14-16 (KJV)

I don't glow in the dark either. And then there is this . . .

> Now the earth was formless and empty, darkness was over the surface of the deep, and the Spirit of God was hovering over the waters. And God said, "Let there be light," and there was light. God saw that the light was good, and he separated the light from the darkness. God called the light "day," and the darkness he called "night." And there was evening, and there was morning—the first day. —NIV Genesis 1:2-3

The modern believer's mind begins to work and seek a simple resolution. "The light of the first day is 'real light' The other verses about light are metaphorical." Further along we read on the fourth day God created the lights in the sky to mark of the seasons, the sun and the moon. We attempt another scientific reconciliation. "Light was created before God made it into the sun, moon and stars." That is probably true.

Yet among many Jews today and Jews in Jesus' day there's no need for an explanation. The light of the sun and the moon are more the metaphors. The first day's light is something akin to the whole idea of enlightenment. God separates the light from the darkness. The act of separation gives us a definition and meaning. If everything is light and God is everything (pantheism) then the the words 'light' and 'God' are totally meaningless. Light is the very essence of truth: its beauty, its practicality, its eternity. In the Biblical worldview photons enlightening our path through the woods is in the same category as the wisdom that keeps you along the straight and narrow path of virtue and eternal happiness. When you read that Jesus is the light of the world for people living in darkness don't think about the word "metaphor." To walk safely you need the light of God just as much as you need the light God created on the fourth day.

Seeing the Unseen

Psalm 104 is another description of creation:

> Bless the LORD, O my soul. O LORD my God, you are very great. You are clothed with honor and majesty, wrapped in light as with a garment. You stretch out the heavens like a tent, you set the beams of your chambers on the waters, you make the clouds your chariot, you ride on the wings of the wind, you make the winds your messengers, fire and flame your ministers. You set the earth on its foundations, so that it shall never be shaken. You cover it with the deep as with a garment; the waters stood above the mountains. —Psalm 104: 1-6

At creation what was God wearing? "Honor and majesty." In the poetic parallelism common to Hebrew poetry honor and majesty is defined as "light" The sun and moon reflect the glory of the Lord. In lesser and greater degrees the law of God (Psalm 119:105), Jesus, the lilies of the fields and the church do too.

Keeping that thought in mind, how do we fix our eyes on what is "unseen" as 2 Corinthians commends? At night you turn on the electric lights to see. Outside the stars and the moon give you enough light to see the world in black and white. As the sun, the greater light, rises the grays fade, the color returns. The sun gives us knowledge where to walk in our world. The Bible tells us that without the moon and the sun we stumble around. But we also stumble and fall without the wisdom of the law, without "the light of men." Isaiah 59:10 says, "We grope for the wall like the blind, and we grope as if *we had* no eyes: we stumble at noonday as in the night; *we are* in desolate places as dead *men*."(KJV)

In our present enlightened, scientific age, we envision 'light' as solar or electric photons bouncing off not-so-dark matter. Science Fiction fans of *Star Trek* may think of deadly photon torpedoes crossing the dark void of space at far less than the speed of light. Visible light is just a part of what we and the Bible means by 'light.' *Light* is anything that helps us find our way through life and even along "the valley of the shadow of death." Light is any thing, any thought, any idea that helps us to live. Light is more than bands of energy along the electromagnetic wavelength.

In many languages "light' is a fun word. In cartoon and comic strip art light bulbs pop over characters' heads. We know that a mind has generated a plan of action or a scheme of revenge. The brighter the light bulb the better the idea. Villains and unsympathetic characters have small ideas. They appear "unenlightened."

Scientific discoveries bring enlightenment. Gurus and safron-robed monks claim the same. Some mystics, doctors, politicians, and even preachers walk around with heads held high as enlightened leaders of today's generation. God created the light, not them. They parade around like the new Moses leading us to a promised land (Freud actually saw himself as the new Moses for a post-Christian modern era.). Their seminars and book tables may merit our attention. But we must use discernment. They may be frauds. We can't tell the wheat from the weeds. Only God can judge hearts. Just as often enlightened leadership can show a bit of the dark side.

In one moment of vanity a politician with many good ideas mocked Pennsylvania opponents of big government as bitter and clinging to "guns or religion." It was surely a moment of 'unenligtenment.' At the time I remember thinking . . .

> Wait a minute? Aren't bitter people more agnostic/atheistic than Jewish/Christian? If a man puts a knife to my throat and wears a "God is dead" t-shirt should I feel safe? Am I in greater danger if I park next to a car with a dead deer on the roof and 'Jesus loves you' sticker on the rear bumper? Didn't the founding fathers also fear big, intrusive government? Doesn't Christianity kick against the soapbox of all powerful emperors and dictators? Isn't religion one of the checks and balances of our national identity?

That was a verbal meditation. I also imagined the thief jumping into my car. I shout to him, "Thank you for being an atheist and keeping guns off the streets."

Many older people complain that America is too divided, not as friendly as it used to be. Comedy news programs with strong political or religious intentions mock alternative views as unenlightened. The condescension is without reasoned explanation. The political and religious indecorum of *Saturday Night Live* reigns. We are left with sound bites not insights. More heat than light comes out of flat screen TV's. Our minds/hearts gain confidence in our cause without further knowledge or unenlightened. There are places for sarcasm but only when it encourages us all to learn more.

When we don't know we are "in the dark." Light, no matter what form it takes, must enter our minds through our senses. Every generation begins in ignorance and must continue to grow up in wisdom and knowledge. We grow not for vanity's sake but in order to face the challenges of employment, marriage, parenting and death. It doesn't matter the light source: sunlight; psychology, a painting, an audio book, a family photograph, preaching or a good novel. They all can have light. But it's not light/enlightenment until it gets into our heads and we start thinking Wisdom and creativity starts with a voice originating in our heads, the very heart of who we are.

Seeing with our Hearts

What thoughts or images come to mind when you think about thinking? Before Sigmund Freud introduced us to the libido and unconscious, we measured character by conscious thoughts and actions. Shakespeare and the great playwrights gave us the soliloquy to hear the heart of characters. Nineteenth century novelists were masters of the dialogue enabling us to fathom the heart of human nature. Now we prefer another way. We want color, action and entertainment. The consequences are shallow answers to complicated problems. We lack serious meditation about difficult problems. Like Polonius in Shakespeare's *Hamlet*, we prefer to think and speak in moral, political and religious cliches: "Above all to thine own self be true" (Shouldn't we also be true to others?). We've lost or at least enfeebled the Divine art of thinking and understanding.

Stop the videos. Parents and teachers like to entertain their students and children with a good movie. It gives them a time to relax, correct papers, cook supper and do every thing but vacuum the floor. But is it too much of a good thing? Do children and students have enough time to take it all in and understand?

The educational DVD goes quickly by. The boys in class want adrenaline soaked movies; the girls want romance and song. It's not like the first bottle of champagne. They have already seen a dozen hours of TV and videos during the weekend. There's no magic. The girls think music; the boys think games. The video educational moment is rated as a tasteless box of vitamin-fortified cereal. The teachers complain that the students aren't reading. So the class sees a movie, not read a book. Facts are memorized but not understood. There's no meditation.

Mom and Dad don't talk much. The have lost the will or wisdom to engage in entertaining conversation. The only thing to talk about is paying the bills. They watch everything together. They have nothing uncommon to share. There's no meditation.

In the college lounge students stare at everything that moves on the TV screens. They don't have the time or patience to read Shakespeare. *The Simpsons* are on the tube. Everyone stops and stares. They know which professors are easy; which don't check for plagiarism.

In another part of the city, in another university, students attack the textbooks like Marines storming the beaches of Tarawa. The textbook pages don't flicker by. They master each page before they go on to the next. Just before the exam they open the book again, scan notes and review. Their homes are training centers for learning. TV and web surfing is not 24/7. They pray for wisdom. They wish to honor their parents by attending an elite institution. They are Korean. Their hearts are filled with something of value . . . a good education. Later they talk about what they learned. There's meditation. But it must be coupled with Christian desire to seek truth and light. Getting to Harvard or Emery University is not the measure of honor for students, virtue is.

I want more light that is more than daylight. Pointing my camera to the east, I got a spectacular photo of the sun rising above the South China Sea. I wanted to hold that memory long enough to enjoy it later. My JPG picture file recorded the time as 7:45 AM January 23, 2004 . I shot the picture from a quiet hotel on the side of a hill, just west of the city of Lingshui, Hainan Island, China. The next day I climbed a higher hill to watch the sun setting over the island. I've watched sunrises and sunsets in China and the USA. I know that joyous longing described by famed writer C. S. Lewis. Whether I watched the interplay of light and darkness from the White Mountains of New Hampshire or at the rim of a Pacific volcano, I never saw a cat or dog there, enjoying the same view. Some people don't see the joyous beauty either. I meditate and wonder why so few of us see how good it is.

Today it's hard for us to see the glory that awaits us beyond the sunset. After hundreds of Christian missionaries were massacred during the China's Boxer Rebellion of 1900 the number of Americans volunteering to serve increased. Today very few mega-church leaders take martyrdom seriously. Serving God in obscurity on the mission field and awaiting the rewards of Heaven are not in keeping with pop culture's impatience and love of fame. I understand that even church leaders face temptations, yet too many suffer from scandal. They are less willing to suffer the cross. They don't see the joy that awaits them (Hebrews 12:2). Why?

Some studies indicate that sixty and seventy year-old's have more joy than the under thirty something generation. I think that is true. Yet there are also grumpy old men and women. Why? Sometimes it's a brain disorder. It's more likely the memories we chose to treasure in our hearts that determine happiness. Dark images captivate the souls of the bitter.

Seeing the Unseen

Memories also give us light. Survivors of near death disasters say, "I saw my life pass before me." I'm not sure they saw these life memories during or after the crisis. Survivors of airline crashes generally talk more about being afraid and praying than recollecting childhood. People dying slowly think more about their past. They have the free time to meditate on the moments they captured and can recall. They meditate on the memories and judge what in life is good.

There's just not enough enough time to see their whole life pass before them. It is likely that a relatively small quantity of treasured images/memories came to mind. A few years ago I had a near, near death experience. I was enjoying dinner with my wife at a second floor pizzeria in Haikou City, Hainan, China. A fire broke out on the first floor. The smoke was coming up the stairs. Then I saw tall flames climbing up the glass windows.

I had a reason to fear. A year earlier a first floor fire ended in the deaths of a dozen people in another second story restaurant in the nearby city of Sanya. I had seen its blackened windows. According to news accounts the tragedy could have been averted. The dead waited for someone to tell them to leave.

My wife Sherry was sure that it was safe to run quickly out the front door. But the smoke was thick. I knew that smoke can hide flames. I asked the waiter where the fire exit was. There was none. The city either had no fire exit codes or the codes were neglected. From one waiter I learned that there were stairs in a closet that led to the roof. The cooks climb the stairs to take grease and garbage outside. Another man and I encouraged patrons and workers to take to this exit. But the restaurant staff just stood there waiting for a phone call from the owner. It was bizarre, seeing the cooks and bartender shrouded in smoke and overhead lighting just standing at their stations. Their eyes shifted back and forth, not knowing whether to leave or, according to communist tradition, to wait for orders.

The closet was even thicker with smoke. The stairwell had become a chimney. I couldn't see. My wife grabbed my hand to help. I nearly lost my shoe and my balance. I told her to go on, not to worry about me. For the briefest of moments I had memories of my three children and hearing George Beverly Shea sing at the 1964 Billy Graham Boston Crusade. They were my treasured memories. If the risk had been greater and I had more time, I'm sure I'd have remembered my parents and three sisters. The number of memories would be far greater. But we were on the roof in less than a minute. We jumped over to the next building and made our way down another set of stairs and out to the street. The restaurant staff came out ten minutes later, coughing and crying, but without permanent damage. The danger had been minimal. The fire was caused by an electrical short in the sign that hung outside across the entire length of the facade. Only a small portion of the first floor caught fire. The smoke, not the fire, penetrated into the pizza restaurant.

We are collectors of thoughts and memories. Young children get hungry for answers. At three and four-years they start asking "why," "why" and "why." The children don't know why they ask. But neurology and our own experiences tell us that it has something to do with a dramatic change in their language skills. Their awareness and consciousness has expanded and they want it filled. Their hearts are like empty stomachs crying, "I want answers." During the junior high school years parents wonder why they don't ask. Their minds are more like sealed barrels that persist in leaking common sense. For many, learning snaps back in high school or college. I haven't stopped asking, "Why?"

Just think for a moment. Picture in your mind a sunset. Think about a happy time with your family or an old neighbor (If you don't know anyone over thirty then find one.). Think about the last book that made you think. Why do the sunsets give us joy? Why can we read a book or recollect the past with sight and sound somewhere in our heads?

When you read this book do you hear a voice inside? Is it yours? Or someone else? Philosophers, theologians, and neurologist have been trying to answer these questions for centuries. The neurologist searches for neurons and asks if our questions and answers are healthy or dysfunctional. The

Seeing the Unseen

philosopher finds a variety of answers and then adds more questions. The theologian wonders if the questions point the way to a temporary or eternal destination.

I don't have a degree in Medicine. Neurological answers are above my pay grade. The data collected by science is never any good by itself (The joy of marriage can not be contained in a chapter in a Health Science textbook. The answers are more in the enjoying and in the sharing.). The joy of gazing at a sunset, great conversations over coffee, reading good books, and moments of compassion fill our minds with something beyond rocket science. Memorable musical scores, paintings, photographs, private memories linger in our consciousness. If God seekers are right they indicate character and reveal temporary and eternal destinies.

From the time I was about nine years I have been trying to understand thinking. How is it that I have a voice outside and one inside? Why is that some experiences cast a long shadow in my memory. I try to read six books a month. Yet there's a handful of books I love to read over and over again. I love art and art books. I have visited art museums in Asia, the United States and England. Yet there is a mere handful of paintings that stick onto the walls of my memory palace. In China I got bored with Chinese TV and watched many English language DVD's. I still own many. There's about a dozen or so that I meditate upon and enjoy watching many times (*It's a Wonderful Life* is one; *Pulp Fiction* is not.). I am over sixty and have a large collection of memories. Yet there's just a handful that I enjoy and that linger for a long time.

We can hold only a few memories in our minds at any one time. We all have a few favorite movies, songs and a few favorite books. But how do our minds decide?

The answer is connected with our passion and with our character. Within the Shakespeare's play *Hamlet* (Act 3 Scene 2), King Claudius watches a play called *The Mousetrap*. I dare says it's a play he will remember till his dying day. Neither did David forget Samuel's parable of the sheep. The play, the book, the movie that lingers are about us. The psychologist

Seeing the Unseen

Hermann Rorschach (1884 - 1922) wanted to read people's minds. Because Freudian psychology sees much of the mind as unconscious, Rorschach devised a method to read in an indirect, unconscious manner. He used blots of ink on paper. Today's psychologists ask clients what they see in the inkblots. It is like looking up at the clouds with a friend and sharing what you see. The difference is that the psychologist have black clouds that don't change with every passing wind.

For purposes of a security clearance in the military I was once tested with ten inkblots.

"It's a dissected brain." That was my answers for one of them. I know why I saw that. Inkblots were made by dripping ink on absorbent paper and then folding the paper once. It creates bilateral images. The brain is also bilateral. I knew the psychologist was trying to 'objectively' pick my brain apart. That inkblot image wasn't testing my subconscious at all. It was merely measuring my assessment of the test. If I had recently watched a Bruce Willis film I might say, "I see dead people."

The tool and the interpretation is hardly mathematical science. At times the test does measure what is important to us, what we meditate on. Sometimes it just measures recent experiences.

My older sister took the test too. She did better than I.

"I saw ink spots. That's what I told him. They were all just ink spots. Then he got angry. I think he was nuts."

His response may mean that he had unconscious hostilities or a lack of self-control. More than black spots, the memories we hold dear, the choice of books, the arts we love, the music we enjoy are signs of our unique experiences, education, and cognitive skills and the meditations of our hearts.

But why do we think and see images in the clouds and ink spots? Why do we think about our past? Why is there a little voice inside my head? Jews, Christians and anyone living within Western Culture know something about the Bible. There's a verse with cosmic proportions that draws a picture of our ability to think and exceed the intelligence of our nearest biological neighbor. Moses wrote these words to ponder . . .

And God said, Let us make man in our image, after our likeness .and let them have dominion over the fish of the sea, and over the fowl of the air, and over the cattle, and over all the earth, and over every creeping thing that creepeth upon the earth.
    So God created man in his own image, in the image of God created he him; male and female created he them.

You have probably read and diagnosed these words of Scripture a number of times. But what exactly does it mean to be in the *image of God*?

Chapter Two

Defining the Image

Not Male and Female

Recently I listened to a PBS program entitled "Bill Moyers; Genesis a Conversation." A group of writers and religious leaders got together to talk about the first book of the Bible. Some thought the image of God as male and female.

Really? This can only be called city talk. Even a child knows that there is a rooster and a hen. A little older and children know that there are rams and ewes. Certainly by the end of junior high school the educated know that there are male and females chickens, male and female sheep. When God commanded Noah to place in the ark "male and female" Noah knew the difference. Perhaps the Bill Moyers' discussion group was searching more for a god for equal pay and equal protection.

Making Male and Female Images Divine.

If our divine image is as male and female then when do we most reflect that identity? Ages one to twelve? Ages thirteen to forty? Ages forty to sixty? To find the American answer just pick up any magazine or see the sexual focus of pop advertising. It's

Seeing the Unseen

---

about youth. With age the original biological purpose of sex: procreation is . . . ah, less urgent.

There are other consequences for making sexuality a measure of divinity. Children are trivialized until they become mature or costumed to look provocatively older. Advertisers fixate more on male and female plumage, less on the wisdom and the long-term joy that can't be marketed. In the 1940's and 50's public culture much less identified individuals by sexual orientation or activity. Modesty prevailed. Today the phrase "older and wiser" has been replaced by "old and out of step." The elderly are losing their outward sexual identity of smooth skin and firm shape. They have become marginalized. Their wisdom is segregated into nursing homes, supermarket aisles and bus depots. We keep them waiting for a phone call or a knock on the door from a neighbor, children and grandchildren. The hip-hop generation are too too busy to come and talk, listen and learn.

Does the Bible say we are created in the image of God as male and female? To the contrary The Bible is standing virtuously against this pagan tradition. Contrary to many religions, Genesis says that the divine image is not "just for men" or "for women only." The image is in evidence at age twenty-one and at eighty-one.

Michelangelo's *David* stands seventeen tall. It's one of the grand attractions of Florence, Italy, an unquestionable art masterpiece. Yet, why is it nude? Why is this colossal not circumcised? David is Jewish. Michelangelo and his patrons knew the anatomical difference between Italian and Jewish boys. Holding a sling over his shoulder and calling the statute 'David' does not make it Biblical. Its image is more Roman than Jewish. In

23

Seeing the Unseen

Greco-Roman art figures in pottery, marble and concrete, are young and athletic. The male figure is close in shape to the mythical gods. Youthful, athletic animation was synonymous with the divine. The colossal Greek and Roman statutes were icons honoring Olympians with six-pack abs. The Greeks and Romans measured life by athletics less by love and compassion. Hercules is athletic, a divine man. The real David was young and diminutive compared to Goliath.

But that is not rest of the story. Michelangelo's *David* is now out of place. It was intended to stand on a buttress of the Florence Cathedral where the large armies surrounding the city can see the heart of the people of Florence: naked determination. The torso is purely classical, a devotion to youth and sexuality. Yet the face is the face of David and everyone with a just cause facing a powerful enemy. It is a Lexington and Concord minuteman facing the might of the British Army. It's a black soldier of the 54th Massachusetts Regiment preparing to charge Fort Warren in 1863. It's a civil rights worker determined to liberate America from segregation and white-only or black-only brotherhoods. It is honorable service men and women protecting Islamic order and civility from being devoured and overturned by Islamic chaos. It is the Jew and the Christian refusing to surrender faith and civility in the valley of the shadow of death. It is the face of Great Britain and the Royal Air Force facing the larger, Nazi aerial armada. With a little imagination David has bulldog jowls and a cigar in his mouth inspiring England in its finest hour. Look closer. Use your imagination. It is the face of Anne Frank who refuses to surrender to the twin evils of hatred and cynicism.

Seeing the Unseen

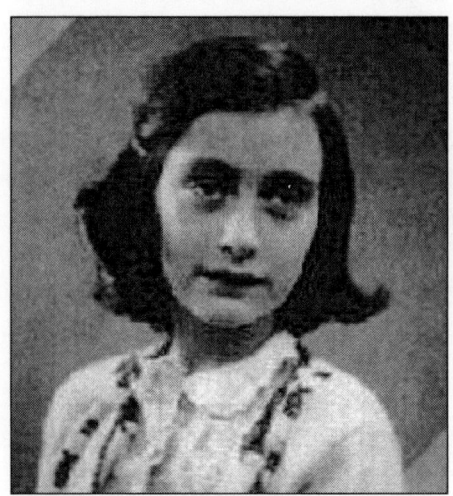

In keeping with a humanity created in the image of God, the real David's great worth is measured more on the meditations of his heart. In poetry David celebrated the glory of God in nature. His poetry projects upon the page his heart's confession and confrontation with sin. In Psalm 139:23f David says, "Search me, O God, and know my heart: try me, and know my thoughts: And see if there be any wicked way in me, and lead me in the way everlasting." (Psalm 139 KJV) If Jesus had attained an Olympian wreath he would have been immortalized in Greek marble and Roman concrete only. Instead His character is etched on human hearts.

Humanity, in the image of God, is neither male nor female; it is nether left-handed nor right-handed. There are no Scriptures suggesting that our divine likeness is implemented by X and Y chromosomes. In some cultures divinity is more masculine. Other religions see it in reproductive females and their 'powerful and magical' womb. Genesis speaks against such sexual discrimination. God bestows the very same divine uniqueness and blessings on both.

European- Americans often fail to see the "sexually sanctioned prejudices" in Asian and African religions. Tibetan Buddhism is a good example. Steven Seagal, a powerful martial arts actor, was declared to be a *tulku*, a reincarnation of a dead lama.[1] How was the choice made? Was it his testosterone or fan idolatry that was a sign of his past lamaist life? Why not name a Tibetan woman who has been praying before a statue of Buddha for the last fifty years? Was this a sexually biased decision? Tibetan Buddhism assigns demonic powers to the land of Tibet herself. The land is a demoness held in check by Buddhist shrines and temples. Of late Tibetan Buddhist women have come to prominence. Yet their honor and notoriety are largely outside of Tibet.

And who is most in the image of God? Story teller Hans Christian Anderson reminds us that the clearest image of God and His glory may be an old granny. Even Judaism, Christendom's ancestral and theological predecessor, honors great women of faith. God judges the heart. The great Jewish-Yiddish storyteller Sholem Aleichem (1859-1916) ponders the thought that the most blameless of Jews might be a mute, unpaid coachman like Bontche Schweig. For both faiths there is no undiscovered reincarnation awaiting discovery. We don't look for a hidden imam either.

Rene Descartes famously quipped, "I think therefore I am." The 1960's Woodstock Generation had its own, sexually vulgar version. Yet the pious Rene Descartes would be pleased to know how close he was to the Biblical understanding of our divine image. It's not in our loins; it's in our thinking. Our thinking exceeds the rationality of our ape and dolphin neighbors by cosmic proportions.

After saying all that I acknowledge that a certain degree of male and femaleness in the divine image. It's not about sexual impulses. It's about two ways of thinking becoming one. It's a husband submitting his plans and ideas to his wife; it's a wife doing the same.

The Koran on God's Image.

I am a great admirer of the late Pakistani leader Benizar Bhutto. Her outspoken defense of Islam is one of the best. She was well aware that early Islamic kings like Mali's, Mansa Musa (1312—1337) provided better protection of women than pagan, North African traditions. But Bhutto's rendition of Islam is not the religion of the Quran alone. Bhutto studied at both Harvard and Oxford. Her education was in secular universities preserving Greek and Judeo-Christian assumptions. The Islam she defends is the enlightened Post-Quranic philosophy forged in the cosmopolitan culture of the former Byzantine Empire. Her defense of Islamic woman's rights relies more upon Christian consensus than Qur'anic admonition.

In Surah 4:34 men are given the right to hit their wives. Here's an English translation from a defender of Islam, M. A. S. Abdel Haleem:

> If you fear high-handedness from your wives, remind them [of the teachings of God], then ignore them when you go to bed, then hit them.

Haleem footnotes that "hit"in context means a single blow. But his translation says "wives." Is that one blow for each wife?[2]

Later, in the same Surah, at verse 128, there is a wife's protection against "high-handedness" from one husband. Yet there is no parallel mention of hitting. Why? The reason is not spiritual but physical. She is no match to her husband's fists. Men are generally physically stronger. Different hormones create a different muscle-to-fat ratio. They cause more fear and physical harm. Battered husbands are rare. Because God is the all powerful creator the Qur'an and other religions assume that men are more godly than women. In contrast to verse thirty-four, verse 128's subject and predicate are in the singular not the plural. The Qur'an accepts the right of a man to have more than one wife but not the reverse. Islam inscribes a God that is aloof, distant, expressive more of divine power than divine love. He is an aloof, distant father figure. In contrast the Bible considers men and women different but without sexual superiority. God is not macho; nor is He a hermaphrodite: both female and male.

Not Power Theology

Look at another possible definition of "image of God." The image is of dominion:

> *And let them have dominion over the fish of the sea, and over the fowl of the air, and over the cattle, and over all the earth, and over every creeping thing that creepeth. upon the earth.*
>
> *-Gen 1:26b KJV*

There is the Dominion theory. We are in the image of God because we have authority or "dominion" over the earth. According to this view there is a certain morality in controlling the land and all the wildlife. Putting animals in cages, shooting lions and toppling the largest of trees are God's intent for us.

Some have gone so far as to "claim the ground" and try to take authority over governments, churches and even other Christians they regard as inferior . . . all in the name of God. But how do we exercise authority over all the earth? Like Obi-wan Kenobi in the film *Star Wars*, do we use the (Spirit) force to control the simple minds of animals and politicians? Perhaps humans can have more of nature's *chi*, like Daoists, Neoconfusianists and pop cultists seem to think.

There is a more natural answer. Just for a moment imagine you are camping alone in the Alaskan woods. There seems to be some movement in the bushes. Suddenly a grizzly bear charges you. In a split second you remember the verse of Scripture and shout, "I have been give authority over all the earth." What happens next?

It's a foolish and scary. Yet we do have dominion over the Grizzly bear, the great Alaskan Brown Bear. Our authority over such animals is not by being in the image of God. It is rather the consequences of that divine image.

Seeing the Unseen

To get a clue about how we have authority over animals and over the world. We need to look at a not so great hunter:

Elmer Fudd:

And his prey and nemesis:

Bugs Bunny

Seeing the Unseen

Why do we love their cartoon antics? They act the opposite of what we expect. The rabbit dominates; the man. Elmer Fudd is befuddled. He doesn't seem to learn anything. He tries the same thing over and over again. The rabbit talks and talks. Bugs reads. Bugs gives soliloquies to himself and to the TV/movie theater audience in a streetwise Brooklyn, Flatbush accent. By contrast Elmer is dull of speech and is lost in the woods.

Real rabbits can't think through a problem to find a better solution. A good hunter is creative, He can build the better mouse trap . . . rabbit trap. That's how we have authority over all the earth. We can think through to a solution. It is the key that distinguishes us from all other plants and animals. It is our creative and inventive thinking that enables us to have dominion over all the earth.

In high school textbooks, best sellers and PBS specials we have images of a line of human evolution. The line of progress runs from a tree monkey ascending to a humanity with less jaw bone and hair and an improved posture. But the last mutation in the human species has nothing to do with posture or civil appearance. The final step was a throat reshaped for speech and a brain rewired to think with words. Those two changes are hard to illustrate.

It is the best step of physical evolution. With a brain there is no need for multi-genetic mutations. We soar higher than any eagle, travel faster than the cheetah and swim deeper and farther, without changing our genes. Viruses can survive by mutating in a matter of a season or two. Man survives by learning and educating the next generation. We can change our environment, creating better domiciles, better textiles and better bodies. Atheism is not a higher state of evolution, as some suggest. Nor is religion. Whenever we face the four horsemen of the Apocalypse; conquest, war, famine and death; we don't evolve. We adapt through scientific innovation, reasoned philosophy and a mind set on the sacred duty of compassion and virtue.

Man can out-think other animals. But how? We are smarter. We are clever. That doesn't say much. How are we smarter and clever? It's not a matter of more brain cells per body mass. It's more about how our brains are different. The answer Genesis one gives is so close to us that we often miss it. The answer that is so "on the money" that even a cynical atheist might say "Amen."

The solution to man's thinking superiority and dominion over the animals is in who God is.

Genesis 1:26 & 27 says:

> *And God said, Let us make man in our image, after our likeness .and let them have dominion over the fish of the sea, and over the fowl of the air, and over the cattle, and over all the earth, and over every creeping thing that creepeth upon the earth.*
>
> *So God created man in his own image, in the image of God created he him; male and female created he them.*

In the image of God? Which God? There were a few choices available to Moses and his twelve tribes . . .

There's Anubis or *Sekhem Em Pet.* Anubis is the god of the dead. It is he that opens the crypt and releases the dead from sleep. For his worshipers he tips the scale on judgment day and assures rebirth.

Anubis is shown as a jackal or a man with a jackal's head. There's an interesting reason why Anubis became connected with the dead. Most ancient Egyptians could not afford elaborate tombs or pyramids. Instead they were buried in the necropolis, the city of the dead. Wild jackals trotted about its streets. Sometimes they were seen scratching at the door of the tombs or digging into the graves. To a pet owner from Memphis, Egypt this seemed like loyalty, the loyalty of a grieving family member wanting to see the dead alive again. But these jackals are no pets. They're wild animals. It is not loyalty displayed. It's hunger. Dogs have a nose for flesh and decaying meat.

We are certainly not in the image of jackals. Instead we take authority even over wild dogs and train them to be in our image. We discipline their diets to prefer chicken more than mummy wraps. We train them to accept Alpo and not Al for dinner.

Seeing the Unseen

Not the God that Glitters.

Here are two other gods . .

Both these gods are idols. The lady on the left is Selket. She is a goddess who protects people from scorpion bites. She wears a scorpion on her head. She's a handy god to have in Egypt, if she really works her magic. The North African Scorpion is the deadliest in the world. The Golden Calf arose out of our lawless nature and impatience with God and with Moses. The real God didn't move fast enough. So the Hebrew people engraved an image of God that moves just as freely and as fast as they wanted 'it' to do. But a Golden calf, even a bull market isn't the source of happiness. Moses' God call us to wait and follow Him. Idols are images of things here on the earth; we are images of God in Heaven. Gold is a rare element; but the divine image is universal.

There is a reason why so many idols are covered in gold. Of all natural materials gold and diamonds reflect light. There were no diamonds in the Middle East in Biblical times. There was much gold in royal palaces. In the Bible the sun symbolically reflects God as light to the world. Gold is therefore a reflection of a reflection of God. A bit of gold attracts our attention. But by covering a wooden object entirely of gold we make an idol shimmering and godlike.

In the great poem *Paradise Lost*, John Milton speculates on how Satan could have fallen from Heaven. This angel fell in love with the streets of gold more than whose light gives the gold its dazzle:

> From heav'n, for ev'n in heav'n his looks & thoughts
> Were always downward bent, admiring more
> The riches of Heav'ns pavement, trod'n Gold,
> Then aught divine or holy else enjoy'd
> In vision beatific: by him first
> Men also, and by his suggestion taught,
> Ransack'd the Center, and with impious hands
> Rifl'd the bowels of their mother Earth
> For Treasures better hid.

Milton was not a fan of kings wrapped in pearls, ermine and majestic gold. He preferred an educated nation devoted to republican democracy. He believed in a nation without divine kings or leaders who declared a divine right apart from the natural law.

There's much truth in Milton's poem. The devout are less interested in gold than God's more rebellious children. Rebels prefer idols to look "fabulous" in gold, diamonds and all that glitters. But think for moment. Did Elvis sing any better when he wore his gold suit? Do the number of gold chains a man or woman wears indicate greater virtue or talent? We know the answer. Yet we are seduced by the color of the finery and pop's devotion to the lifestyle of the rich and the famous. Ella Fitzgerald (1918-1996) was not a beauty queen. She didn't politicize her sexuality. She dressed modestly. If you close your eyes and listen, to her vocals and that of Miley, Britney or Madonna, your ear, the ultimate judge of music, tells who's the real queen of pop—*doo-ah, dooooo-aaaaah.*

What is most wondrous about listening to Ella's recordings is the resurrection factor. Your heart sees no benefit by distinguishing between a deceased voice on a recording and a live voice on your cell phone. Jesus, Shakespeare, Anne Frank Homer, Virgil, and Abraham Lincoln's voices come into our hearts just as clear—sometimes clearer than a pop novelist with gold on his fingers and in his pockets. God regards us living or dead with the same love—with the same worth. Christians and Jews therefore are to regard the neighbor and the nemesis, president or plumber with the same care and compassion. It is a great loss for the living if we neglect great words coming from the membership of the dead writers, singers, and poets society.

There are no pop gods among us. We are all in the image of God. Which God are we in the image of? How are we to protect ourselves from creating a God in the image of an animal or a less than perfect person? First by reading Genesis as a good piece of literature. You may remember your high school English teacher telling you about pronouns. If the school essay you handed in for an assignment did not make clear the meanings of all your 'he's,' 'she's' and "it's" it was not well written. Your teacher would remind you in red pencil that pronouns are indefinite. You must have an antecedent. The word "god" is very much like a pronoun. The indefinite term "God" in the phrase "image of God" must be defined before we can define ourselves. The definition is there in what precedes the verse that says we are "in the image of God."

Chapter Three

The Genesis of Who We are and Who We Ought to Be

When I first read Genesis I was unaware that most fundamentalists and atheists take it as an ancient scientific narrative. The former see it as good science, the latter as pseudoscience. I knew nothing of the scholars who interpret Genesis as just another creation myth. I just read from one of the more poetic and literary articulate of versions, the King James.

At sixteen I had already read Coleridge, Whitman, Houseman, Frost and heard the pathetic love songs of the 50's and 60's. My high school teachers taught me that history and science are more about facts. But Poetry is more about feelings and what an author wants us to feel <u>after</u> something has happened. A good example is in Moses' song <u>after</u> God's victory:

> Then sang Moses and the children of Israel this song unto the LORD, and spake, saying, I will sing unto the LORD, for he hath triumphed gloriously: the horse and his rider hath he thrown into the sea.
>
> The LORD *is* my strength and song, and he is become my salvation: he *is* my God, and I will prepare him an habitation; my father's God, and I will exalt him.
> Ex 15:1b-2KJV

Later in graduate school I learned that the first chapter of Genesis has characteristics in common with the poetry of the Book of Psalms: repetition of phrases, parallel structure; as well as marks of narrative. It is narrative poetry, poetry with a story. What then does Moses, the inspired author of the creation story, want us to feel?

A modern event helps to illustrate the intent of Genesis one. Do you remember or have seen the televised transmission of Apollo 8 as it orbited around the moon? It was Christmas Eve, 1968. Apollo 8's crew were engineers, test pilots and astronauts. Frank Borman, Jim Lovell, and William Anders read Genesis chapter one from the King James Version. They read it just as the spacecraft camera captured light coming from the grey, lifeless surface of the moon and then from a bright, blue earth rise . . .

Ge 1:1 In the beginning God created the heavens and the earth.

Ge 1:2 *And the earth was without form, and void; and darkness was upon the face of the deep. And the spirit of God moved upon the face of the waters.*

Ge 1:3 And God said, Let there be light: and there was light.

Ge 1:4 And God saw the light, that *it was* good: and God divided the light from the darkness.

Ge 1:5 And God called the light Day, and the darkness he called Night. And the evening and the morning were the first day.

Ge 1:6 And God said, Let there be a firmament in the midst of the waters, and let it divide the waters from the waters.

Ge 1:7 And God made the firmament, and divided the waters which *were* under the firmament from the waters which *were* above the firmament: and it was so.

Ge 1:8 And God called the firmament Heaven. And the evening and the morning were the second day.

Ge 1:9 And God said, Let the waters under the heaven be gathered together unto one place, and let the dry *land* appear: and it was so.

Ge 1:10 And God called the dry *land* Earth; and the gathering together of the waters called he Seas:

and God saw that *it was* good.

The Apollo 8 transmission ended with a wish that everyone upon the earth have a Merry Christmas and God's blessing.
    The three men could have just said "Happy Holidays" and given a scientific recitation about gravity, lunar craters, the speed of light and the distance between the earth and the

moon. Instead, they sent to earth a passion best conveyed in poetry. Compared to the stark, barrenness of the moon and all other cosmic landscapes thus discovered the earth is *good*, a blessing from God They chose to recite a spiritual vision. The poetic revelation helped millions to see the unseen.

There is also something to be said about the literary impact of the King James Version. It is the repetition of "and God." Some modern versions have taken out the repetitious "and." Yet the Hebrew word at the beginning of a sentence is something like the English "and then." But there is another possibility. Like the "and" in the Gospel of Mark it is the author's intentional pause. It gives us a little more time to visualize the words. It is the listener's time to make the picture. It's the ancient equivalent of the southern American story teller's "You see." In the early comedy of Andy Griffith, in Jerry Glover's monologues you might hear something like, "You see there was this here......? You *see* the story as you *hear* it. Genesis and The Gospel of Mark both want you to see what you read.

From Genesis 1:3 to verse 10, each line begins with "And God"

And God said

    And God saw

    And God called

And God said

    And God made

    And God called

And God said

    And God called

And God saw

Did you get the picture in your heart . . . in your mind's eye? God is a speaker. He is not some wordless "ground of our being."

You see there is this here God of Abraham, Isaac and Jacob; He's a talker.

Animals don't talk at all. And God doesn't talk his head off, telling what us to do every day, and how to wash our faces. "Don't forget behind the ears." You may may have wished that God told husbands to take out the trash and help with the dishes. You may cry out to God and ask, "Why didn't you command wives, 'Thou shall not shop with your husband nor vacuum on the Day of Superbowl'?" God didn't. Instead God got right to the point. He gave us a heart to think and a command to love. Like God we think with words.

God said and we speak, We take this miraculous, language gift for granted. We can talk. We can write down the words we hear from others and the ones we created in our heads. We share that ability with God alone. God speaks as the author of creation. Man is also an author.

The Language of God's creation is in our midst. Just for a moment imagine you are walking a path in a great forest. There is a great myriad of grasses, ferns, molds, mushrooms, trees, insects, birds and mammals not more than a hundred feet to the left and right of the path. It is a grand library of God's genetically inscribed words. Creationists and evolutionist differ on how many books and how long the chapters are. Both sides agree that it is an enormous gene library. Its exterior is written in the dialect of fractal mathematics; its interior blueprint is in the chemical language of DNA. Secular humanists honor man the reader; theists honor the God the writer. God calls the books "good." God writes books, good books. "And God saw that it was good."

Rube Goldberg and the Image of God.

God's plan of creation is perfect. He doesn't have to make so many late changes. The course and evolution of life was already planned out in words spoken in the beginning.

One of the great, creative cartoonists of the twentieth century was Rube Goldberg (1883-1970). With a touch of mirth about assembly line processing, he created fanciful methods to do simple tasks. In honor of Rube Goldberg engineering students put together even more fantastic devices to the applause of an audience. They publish their inventions on You Tube. Yet It is a quantum step back from the grand plan that created the Heavens and earth and two-legged talkers.

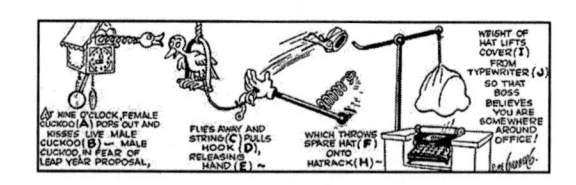

Here are a series of comical connections between the cuckoo clock and the typewriter. No one in his right mind would say that it was by chance that the cuckoo clock lifted the typewriter cover. British Science writer James Burke's documentary series *Connections* (1978, 1994, 1997) showed that scientific discovery, though engineered by scientists, often followed a path much like a Rube Goldberg variation. Over the stretch of time there is a natural progression. Yet at any specific time it seems "quite by chance."

Before there was Goldberg there was God, establishing the most elaborate and detailed of inventions, the evolution of life. Some steps include "Store energy by planting large plants and dinosaurs; throw a big rock and kill all the big dinosaurs." God has some unique Goldberg variations. He allows for human folly and creativity. According to the plan the machine explodes in a fireworks display, a curtain opens to reveal the door to His house and many of the moving parts roll inside. It was of course a master plan that enables God to rest and later for us to do His good will. He didn't have to keep fixing it—unless we ask

In the Heavenly realms the angels must have laughed when they saw how God powered up the dust and created an image of Himself. It was not a short story: "You see I created this here slime, on a rock, in the sea and it moves." Evolution, the most complex of inventions, neither proves or disproves that there is a grand Creator behind the cosmic proceedings. You can see in evolution the finger-play of God or God's absence. The evidence is circumstantial. The human jury is divided between those that seek and see Him, and those that don't.

The evidence is intentionally circumstantial to allow us free will. God allows us to live in a mental Garden of Eden where God is not so clearly present. In our hearts are the words of a loving father who wants us to mature. We hear echoes of the words of the Tempter. What things do we "meditate on" as Psalm 1 warns or what things we "think on" as Paul says in Philippians 4 determines our daily course and our ultimate destination.

In my old age I often see the truth behind the truth in visual images . . . like a cartoon miniseries. In one corner of the mind there's the challenger, Satan. Like a snake he lifts his head up high. He offers the arena audience a life that is grand and fabulous. Of course he can't hold his head high for long. The fearful head keeps falling back to the dust to death.

> "Love that cobra cape, Snake Man. Fabulous! Your fans will just worship you."

> "Thankssss," said the Serpent. "Become one of my kingdom subordinates and people will worship you too."

"Oh, but how?" The young man wonders. His mind is swimming in a mixture of hope that he will and fear that he will not.

"I'm glad you *asp* [sic] that question. It's easy. You've got talent! Above all be sophisticated and arrogant. Deny God, and

Seeing the Unseen

me. Be thoroughly modern, impatient, hate ancient wisdom, and pretend to be wise. Of course you must bear false witness to rise to the top. Smear your political and religious opponents, both foreign and domestic. Let's *seeeee* is there something else? Oh, of course, Tell lies."

"But won't people see through my lies?" Another fame-seeker asks.

"No, no. . . . no. They won't. It's easier than you think. I'll keep them away from books, especially good books. Just salt the truth. Remember: Hide any vindictive bitterness with a knowing, condescending smile. 'Good' garnished with exaggeration and document fabrication will serve your cause."

Satan focuses his stare on another face in the crowd of the self-help seminar. "What's your question?"

"But! What about death? Won't I lose everything when I die?"

"Would I lie to you?" The serpent's head rises higher in a divine pretense. His eyes ablaze with anger that someone would dare question his angelical authority. But a brief moment later, Satan composes himself, backs down from his show of power and gives an assuring smile, "Well, if you insist . . . I will give you everlasting fame, and a guaranteed freedom from judgment. Better yet, a carpet of virgins in heaven for you to enjoy. I am not a hard creature to work with. I'm flexible. After all, I'm a snake."

In the night watches Satan ends his self-help seminar with an epilogue. "Please, everyone. Don't think of the odds. It's Vegas! Hear the liturgy of the state lottery. Megabucks! Play, play. You could be rich, rich! And finally, happy. Take the chance. Real life is Vegas. And, as seen on TV, the happy and young are at the gambling tables. What's to lose? And even if you lose . . . . lose . . . you'll have a fabulous exciting time doing it."

"Here's some great health tips. Men work on those abs. The hot babes will follow. Ladies: tight butts! Remember, TB. Everyone repeat these lines: "I can't believe I'm so lucky."

"I can't believe I'm so lucky."

"You are the most wonderful person in the world. You light up my life."

"You are the most wonderful person in the world. You light up my life."

"Stop! That's all the English you need to know. Remember girls, there are men who are just little boys. They want to play with empty-headed Barbie dolls too."

How come we are so stupid—listening to such nonsense. We have accepted less than perfect relationships and marriages. By focusing on good looks alone we end up in a relationship/marriage made in hell. Some of us have had poor teachers. Parents fail. They let TV and Internet train their children to be lovers and incompetent as friends. In the best and happiest of marriages, the couple are the best of friends. In friendships you share things together and talk. You know enough about your friend to trust. The friendship is close but not close enough to demand change or defeat. You know enough about friendship to successfully share the good times and the bad—"till death us do part." A good friendship has disagreements but not fights or threats.

Satan understands efficiency. If he is to undermine God's glory he first attacks the leadership of countries and the leadership of families. In that way the darkness extends to the next generation and within the unconscious and unthinking followership of national audiences.

Why doesn't God just crush the serpent's head and get rid of that pesky garden snake? He will. But for now he has bound Satan with a long chain that at least limits his power (Jude 1:6; Rev. 20:3). He can no longer deceive entire nations. God calls his children to speak the truth in love. He has prepared a place for us to live, beyond the reach of Satan's power and lies. God has given of Himself. He's given us a Gardner. You know Him. Turn your heart around, just like Mary did on Easter day. You can find Him.

Chapter 3

The Sweet Beauty of Words

※

God speaks. How wondrous is the gift we share with the God of Abraham, Isaac and Jacob. The Library of Congress in Washington, D.C. is across the street from The Capitol Building. It is a work of art. Its windows, sculptures and balustrades honor words and authors. Since 1815 it has been the national treasure of the universal gift of words. It's a forest of some 29 million books, in 490 languages. It stores an even larger number of manuscripts. Recently, America's enemies tried to destroy America by attacking the centers of defense, commerce and trade. Yet closer to their own home they rebel against reason and compassion. They trade drugs for money. The only thing they really fear are books . . . the words and ideas behind America's institutions. The heart of America is not Hollywood or Wall Street. It's the Library of Congress, the public libraries, and down to the private family library of treasured books. Libraries are 'good' places, but not all the leaves of the trees are good for the heart and the soul.

The heart of God is also language. Psalm 139:15f says, "My frame was not hidden from you when I was made in the secret place. When I was woven together in the depths of the earth, your eyes saw my unformed body. All the days ordained for me were written in your book before one of them came to be. " The ordered fashioning of the human body in the womb, "the secret place" is already written down. God's language of DNA dictated that we stand upright. God's word also made us uniquely human by giving us speech neurons, an asymmetrical brain capable of meditation, and a descending hyoid bone for better vocal flexibility.

The DNA code of creation made us in a particular way but also permitted a great variety of skin and hair color, shapes and intelligences. Science and Scripture confirm that much of our own destiny is predestined. It also provides for human freedom. The Author of creation as revealed in science and Scriptures wrote my predestination to be a male. I would not be a mother. But there is the element of free will in determining how many times I will be a father, how many times I would act as a father. Before birth all of humanity was predestined to mature physically. Yet we decide whether we accept the lessons of social maturity. Looking at my family history I may carry the DNA for Alzheimer's or colon cancer. I don't know. Most of us don't have the DNA to protect us from lung cancer, but a few do. We have the freedom to avoid radon gas and tobacco. All of us have DNA that makes us talkers. The destination of the soul train is predestined. It can't jump the tracks. Its destination is not just Heaven, but also to be conformed in the image of his Son (Romans 8:29).

Many Christians and Jews do not see the image of God as language. Why not? Because we are surrounded by language, it comes and goes with our breath. We don't see the trees because we live in the forest. We don't see it until we compare life in the desert.

Compare the sounds of humanity with that of animals.

In *Romeo and Juliet*, Shakespeare creates in written form the silent talk of two hearts. In this famous passage Juliet is silent but we hear Romeo's heart in soliloquy:

> But, soft! what light through yonder window breaks?
> It is the east, and Juliet is the sun.
> Arise, fair sun, and kill the envious moon,
> Who is already sick and pale with grief,

That thou, her maid, art far more fair than she.
Be not her maid, since she is envious;
Her vestal livery is but sick and green
And none but fools do wear it; cast it off.
It is my lady, O, it is my love!
O, that she knew she were!
She speaks yet she says nothing; what of that?
Her eye discourses; I will answer it.
I am too bold, 'tis not to me she speaks.
Two of the fairest stars in all the heaven,
Having some business, do entreat her eyes
To twinkle in their spheres till they return.
What if her eyes were there, they in her head?
The brightness of her cheek would shame those stars,
As daylight doth a lamp; her eyes in heaven
Would through the airy region stream so bright
That birds would sing and think it were not night.
See, how she leans her cheek upon her hand!
O, that I were a glove upon that hand,
That I might touch that cheek!

What language! Is that how you thought when first in love?

And the owls say, "Who-a-who-who."

Winnie the Pooh is a bear. He lives in hundred acre wood. In the author's imagination, Pooh Bear says to his friend Christopher Robin, "If there ever comes a day when we can't be together keep me in your heart, I'll stay there forever." Winnie is not real, but his words are. Both are the creations of British author A. A. Milne.[3]

Real bears don't talk or even growl in conversation with their friends. They live to eat, and they often eat alone. The males don't sit around a deer carcass and "chew the fat."

The Christian essayist and poet Samuel Taylor Coleridge, in a rush on mental inspiration wrote:

Seeing the Unseen

In Xanadu did Kubla Khan
A stately pleasure-dome decree :
Where Alph, the sacred river, ran
Through caverns measureless to man
Down to a sunless sea.
So twice five miles of fertile ground
With walls and towers were girdled round :
And there were gardens bright with sinuous rills,
Where blossomed many an incense-bearing tree ;
And here were forests ancient as the hills,
Enfolding sunny spots of greenery.
But oh! that deep romantic chasm which slanted
Down the green hill athwart a cedarn cover !
A savage place! as holy and enchanted
As e'er beneath a waning moon was haunted
By woman wailing for her demon-lover!
And from this chasm, with ceaseless turmoil seething,
As if this earth in fast thick pants were breathing,
A mighty fountain momently was forced :
Amid whose swift half-intermitted burst
Huge fragments vaulted like rebounding hail,
Or chaffy grain beneath the thresher's flail :
And 'mid these dancing rocks at once and ever
It flung up momently the sacred river.
Five miles meandering with a mazy motion
Through wood and dale the sacred river ran,
Then reached the caverns measureless to man,
And sank in tumult to a lifeless ocean :
And 'mid this tumult Kubla heard from far
Ancestral voices prophesying war !
The shadow of the dome of pleasure
Floated midway on the waves;
Where was heard the mingled measure
From the fountain and the caves.
It was a miracle of rare device,
A sunny pleasure-dome with caves of ice !
A damsel with a dulcimer

Seeing the Unseen

In a vision once I saw:
It was an Abyssinian maid,
And on her dulcimer she played,
Singing of Mount Abora.
Could I revive within me
Her symphony and song,
To such a deep delight 'twould win me,
That with music loud and long,
I would build that dome in air,
That sunny dome! those caves of ice !
And all who heard should see them there,
And all should cry, Beware ! Beware !
His flashing eyes, his floating hair !
Weave a circle round him thrice,
And close your eyes with holy dread,
For he on honey-dew hath fed,
And drunk the milk of Paradise.

And the rooster says, "Cockle-doodle-do."
    A mockingbird has decided to have dominion over my back yard. While his bride nests he protects, sometimes hovering by me, making menacing gestures. I don't mind his fluttering threats. He chortles his domesticity with a delightful medley of songs by bluebirds, cardinals and flycatchers.

But another creature, this one in the divine image, speaks a rhapsody of alliteration

    'Twas brillig, and the slithy toves
    Did gyre and gimble in the wabe:
    All mimsy were the borogoves,
    And the mome raths outgrabe.
    "Beware the Jabberwock, my son!
    The jaws that bite, the claws that catch!
    Beware the Jubjub bird, and shun
    The frumious Bandersnatch!"
    He took his vorpal sword in hand;

Long time the manxome foe he sought—
So rested he by the Tumtum tree,
And stood awhile in thought.
And, as in uffish thought he stood,
The Jabberwock, with eyes of flame,
Came whiffling through the tulgey wood,
And burbled as it came!
One, two! One, two! And through and through
The vorpal blade went snicker-snack!
He left it dead, and with its head
He went galumphing back.
"And hast thou slain the Jabberwock?
Come to my arms, my beamish boy!
O frabjous day! Callooh, Callay!"
He chortled in his joy.
'Twas brillig, and the slithy toves
Did gyre and gimble in the wabe:
All mimsy were the borogoves,
And the mome raths outgrabe. —Lewis Carroll

Jesus says,

> "You have heard that it was said to the people long ago, 'Do not murder, and anyone who murders will be subject to judgment.' But I tell you that anyone who is angry with his brother will be subject to judgment. Again, anyone who says to his brother, 'Raca,' is answerable to the Sanhedrin. But anyone who says, 'You fool!' will be in danger of the fire of hell."

And the Lion roars.

Animals articulate sounds out of instinct. In our own particular vocalization we still keep active vestiges of our mammalian nature. For defense, relief of physical pain, and for mating, English speakers pop out such words such as 'stop,' 'ouch,' 'help,' 'shoot,' and a number of single-syllable German vulgarities. These words befit the Greco-Roman deities who lived within the realm of physical pain, fear, and sexual passion.

But the God who spoke the universe into being calls Himself, "I am;" This God suffers pain, not by age or accident, but by love and by choice. He identifies with our pain and illness. The God of Abraham, Isaac and Jacob does not need vocal chords of His own. He has Moses, David, Isaiah, the prophets and Jesus. He speaks through a great cloud of vocal chords that includes such great orators as Everett McKinley Dirksen 1896-1969), Charlton Heston(1923-2008) , Laurence Olivier (1907-1989), Alexander Scourby (1913-1985), James Earl Jones and all of us. Through the written word of inspiration God writes.

Chapter Five

The Heart the Center of our Consciousness

In common with God we have an apparatus essential for true language and creative thinking. The literature of science and philosophy calls it the inner voice, secondary consciousness, or meta-consciousness. The Bible calls it 'the heart.' When you read this book a voice inside your brain is reciting each word. If you read often the voice changes to images and ideas. If you are bored by a lecture or a sermon outwardly, you may be listening to your own lecture or a sermon coming from your heart, the inner man. You could be watching a home movie in the theater of your soul. You may be talking to yourself.

It is almost unfathomable that God talks to Himself. Yet that's what the Bible says. He does that through the conscious organ of the heart. Is it like our heart? Yes and no. Our heart is a reflection of God's heart. The Bible never speaks of animals having hearts. "The heart of a lion" or "Lion-hearted" is an English, Norman idiom (*coeur de leon*). It is not in the Bible. In the Scriptures lions roar and devour. No lion instructed and loved English children during the London Blitz as C. S. Lewis wrote in *The Lion, The Witch and the Wardrobe*. Aslan is Narnian, not English. He's not even "of this world." The Bible says that man and God have a heart not made of flesh.

> The LORD saw how great man's wickedness on the earth had become, and that every inclination of the thoughts of his **heart** was only evil all the time.
>
> The LORD was grieved that he had made man on the earth, and his **heart** was filled with pain. So the LORD said, "I will wipe mankind, whom I have created, from the face of the earth—men and animals, and creatures that move along the ground, and birds of the air—for I am grieved that I have made them."—Gen. 6:5-7 NIV

In the fifth verse we read about man's heart and its inclination to evil. In the next verse we read of God's grieving heart. The seventh verse says "the Lord said." Who is God talking to? Is this an outer speech to angels? If that is so then are also we in the image of the angels? Or, is this an inner speech spoken to some aspect of Himself? Like the creation narratives, God is speaking to Himself. The God of Abraham is closer to a unified person of more than one self, than today's New age, cosmic theologians are willing to admit.

In the sixth verse we read about God's heart and its inclination to pains of love. But the next verse shows a God so angered that he intends to destroy all of humanity. How can this be? Within the heart of God is justice/judgment and mercy and love. His decisions do not come easy. He heart wrestles with them both.

> "How can I give you up, Ephraim? How can I hand you over, Israel? How can I treat you like Admah? How can I make you like Zeboiim? My heart is changed within me; all my compassion is aroused.
>
> I will not carry out my fierce anger, nor will I turn and devastate Ephraim. For I am God, and not man — the Holy One among you. I will not come in wrath." Hos 11:8-9 NIV

Seeing the Unseen

There are answers that the Bible never acknowledges as holy: don't ask, don't doubt, just believe. That view fits well with the Qur'an, but not the Bible. Job struggled to understand the way of God. David, the prophets also sought to understand His mysterious ways. Even Jesus has a heart talk in the Garden of Gethsemane. Genuine, Biblical faith of the Bible asks, "Why."

Why should doubt be a mark of faith? What about seed faith and its promise of blessings? For one thing, God is more like a father and we have minds that can't comprehend His adult ways. But as a God and we as the sheep and goats of his pasture, we can't comprehend death and eternal life either. Like loving children who have a patient Father we ask, "Why?" I have meditating moments of doubt. After briefly exercising doubt my heart's reasoning is stronger in faith.

Only the family of Noah is to be spared. Why? We are not privy to the just judgment of those who died in the flood. We probably know of a subculture so corrupt that it continues from generation to generation. The Hebrew of Genesis 6:5 tells of a society where "every fashioning/creation of heart" was corrupt. God created the idea of a good world in His heart, and then fashioned it into matter and energy . In Genesis 6:5 the children of men create evil in their hearts and fashion chaos. It's as though man endeavors to kick God out of the garden. God's voice becomes silent and invisible the more man becomes blind and deaf. There comes a time when wisdom and goodness are lost for the next generation.

Darwin wrote a book entitled T*he Descent of Man*. He believed the humanity will ascend and defeat the "savage races."[4] Sigmund Freud and Richard Dawkins believe human descent is the mating of man with religion. But Genesis gives a better answer. Descent and ascent is a matter of the heart's imagination. In Noah's day generation after generation had been taught by word and by example to turn to the dark side. God literally had to take them all out of the world of free choice. It is the divine prerogative only. Only the family of Noah is left.

Seeing the Unseen

Is the flood and God's judgment an actual, historical event? Yes, but there is room for synecdoche, a part representing the whole. As C. S. Lewis points the fatality rate of soldiers is 100%. All die but at different times. Recently the last World War One soldier died. In earthly time the last of the Vietnam veterans and my generation will soon die. But in the heart of God there is grace. The word "grace' first appears in the story of God saving Noah and his family from destruction. Noah represents all the righteous of all generations.

At the heart of the problem is not God but man's. It's about seeking the light. It's about meditation and having enough wisdom to guard our hearts:

> Hold on to instruction, do not let it go; guard it well, for it is your life.
> Do not set foot on the path of the wicked or walk in the way of evil men.
> Avoid it, do not travel on it; turn from it and go on your way.
> For they cannot sleep till they do evil; they are robbed of slumber till they make someone fall.
> They eat the bread of wickedness and drink the wine of violence.
>
> The path of the righteous is like the first gleam of dawn, shining ever brighter till the full light of day. But the way of the wicked is like deep darkness; they do not know what makes them stumble.
>
> My son, pay attention to what I say; listen closely to my words.
> Do not let them out of your sight, keep them within your heart;
> for they are life to those who find them and health toAbove all else, guard your heart, for it is the wellspring of life. (Proverbs 4:13-23)

Heart and Brain

How does the heart work? I have read a number of scholars who say the brain creates a heart or a consciousness. Some show a bias to the physical, others to the spiritual.

Some interpret our mind as a computer. Consciousness is an illusion, a form of biologically programmed artificial intelligence. The billions of neurons with their electrical-chemical impulses are just like a computer programmed with Artificial Intelligence (AI) program. Once programmed a modern robot's computer responds to different sounds, carries out a variety of activities, converse and even wear a plastic smile. Even smarter robots have been in our imagination for some time. But as computers become smaller and memory becomes greater, are our robot dreams becoming like the character "Data" in the TV series *Star Trek the Next Generation?* Data has a program of consciousness. The tin woodsman of Oz searching for a heart has been replaced by thoughtful, even romantic androids.

But robots are really heartless. They don't even think. Any action or response is dictated by a binary, mathematical formula. The robot only appears to understand and respond to your language. The robot acts human because your brain interprets it as human. A child loves a stuffed bear because there are enough associations in the face and body texture that the toy bear appears alive and understands what the child says. Information companies have spent millions of dollars to create computer software that can translate Chinese into English. Some of it works quite well. But even with a voice synthesizer the computer still does not understand or think bilingual thoughts.

Successful advertising and political campaigns work in the same way. It's all about statistical data entry, volume and output. Attractive, sugary, images swing voters' tastes to charisma. Political analysts poll the population and discover that the American mind flees the unkempt morose and reflective leadership of an Abraham Lincoln. They prefer someone handsome and with charisma.

Seeing the Unseen

According to the Computer AI model, life is more about automatic responses:

"Good morning."
"Good Morning."

Flower smell: safe
Decay smell: danger

Bird sounds: safe
sudden load bangs: adrenaline, sweat, get ready to run.

Input in and input out. The output is all in the neural programming.
 Dumping the computer model, others see our consciousness within as an entirely biological model. Biologically, think of consciousness and neurons as a fish bowl filled with goldfish. At first dried ground shrimp is distributed evenly on the surface the waters. But if you change the pattern and put more and more food to the left, the fish will soon be more left leaning while waiting for food.
 Humanity lives in a fishbowl, the argument goes. For the sake of speed and efficiency our neurons also shift to meet changes in the outside world. It is not really a free conscious decision it is merely a response to where the food, the jobs and the power are leaning.
 The biological model accepts what philosophers call primary, or animal consciousness as a survival necessity. Any species survives through reproduction. Dogs in heat give off a scent. Humans give off more visual evidence. When a girl's shape changes: males become interested. The deeply feminine shape indicates great success in childbirth and milk production. A pigeon pecks at a lever in a cage. There's a food pellet. He tries it again for another pellet. If the pellets drop randomly he will peck on the lever until his beak cracks. Slot machines work the same way. People become addictive gamblers because they can't think about statistics on their feet but they do see someone getting money out of the machine called a one-armed

Seeing the Unseen

bandit. Give the dog a yummy and he will do his business outside. Let the slot machine give once and the gambler keeps pulling the lever. Give them welfare and more benefits and they will vote for you. Never let them ponder unforeseen consequences, even national bankruptcy. If you advertise, they will buy.

The biological argument does justice to some aspects of human folly, especially when it comes to adolescents. I do not claim supreme knowledge of the female psyche. Yet in junior high I did observe that the boys most resistant to girls entering their circle of friends were also resistant to bathing. They didn't talk to girls and they had a reverse mating call. They used their hands, mouth and armpits to make "flatus" sounds . . . a definite turn off to a girl's cordial smile. In high school some girls had their minds set on boys whose physique were manicured for speed and power. The boys responded by washing their armpits with great regularity. They changed their dance steps and polyester skins, much like the male mating display of the bird of paradise.

The biological image of the mating season is a problem for humanity. The greater the male aviary display the less monogamous the male proves to be. The greater the physical displays the less likely either male or female will be there for the challenge of child-rearing. Biological relationships end with short explosive single syllable words, much like the speechless bark of a dog. It does not spell well for the survival of the species. The survival of a civilization depends just as much on character as it does sexual maturation.

The Working Heart

How does the human heart really work? Think of a number between one and ten. Now ,what is the capital of the Czech Republic? It is near impossible to read these two sentences without listening to a voice inside. (If you were born deaf your language comes in the form of picture and visualized hand gestures.). Most mortals solve math problems by talking to themselves and using finger gestures; some by seeing the numbers in their heads. The ability to read and to think inside our heads creatively is a byproduct of the gift of language. The heart is a grammar and thought laboratory. As Psalm one reminds us it also enables us to compare, meditate, our actions and ideas with that of God's.

Much of the time the heart is a playground for words, thoughts and images. Have you ever stopped to really listen to what your inner conversations sound like? It is hardly scientific or deep meditation. It's more like an engine idling and going nowhere.

> Now where is my keys? I'm going to be late today. Ah, I remember: on the coffee table . . . stop at Starbucks? No. Just had Hainan coffee twenty minutes ago . . . another cup and I'll be dancin' in the office like Fred Astaire. Bank at eleven; coffee shop next door . . . Fred Astair and Ginger Roberts . . . *Green Mile* . . . Tom Hanks and Ron Howard . . . Davinci Code . . . wasted talent . . one birthday card . . . Is Jeff's birthday first or Bruce's? Lock the door . . . 6:50 . . . perfect time for news on the car radio. Get to the office before Paul gets there.

That's just a under a half a minute of self-talk. When I first said these words I had memories and visions somewhere in my head. Images of the past and future displayed even as I looked to put on my shoes, pick up my briefcase, lock the door behind me and head toward my car (When you read my thoughts on this page did you see something?).

Your dog or cat has visual memories too, but they are episodic. They come randomly or because of some sensual stimulus. Without language animals can't ponder the meaning of a particular event or idea. Despite some cutesy cartoons, they don't climb hills to watch the sunset. They feel good about a supper dish and a pat on the head. They can't see that all of creation is good.

Seeing the Unseen

We are human, not because we walk upright or can make simple tools, as the science textbooks I had in the 1960's preached. We are human because we are in the image of God as thinkers. We use a God-given talent to speak with our outer lips and with our inner hearts. It's that inner voice that gives all of us a thinking edge over Bonzo the chimp. You can think about thinking. You can think about your thinking about thinking. Neither the gorilla nor the dolphin can do what Sammy Davis Jr. sang: "the candy man can." The god-given heart is not some candy heart inscribed with romantic passions or John 3:16. In Biblical terminology, It is more like "the still small voice" of God that Elijah heard. It's what philosophers call "reflective awareness," neurologists call "secondary consciousness." Both disciplines use the word "meta-cognition." It is introspection and self-consciousness. To me it's more a concert hall, an art museum, a memorial hall and a temple.

Thinking, the proper use of the heart, requires exercise and discipline. And as adults know well, there are times when our hearts become incapacitated or walk near the abyss of irrationality. Early adolescents think they can make love decisions. Yet their physical brains are undergoing a re-circuiting, a neural metamorphosis, and an explosion of hormones. They need help. The more junior high school students talk to sober, emotionally stable parents and older adults the fewer mistakes made. Communities/churches that don't segregate by age help. Within the counsel of many there is wisdom (Proverbs 11:14). A family having dinner together and limiting the simulated world of computer and mp3 hyperspace is a family that thinks better of themselves and others. There are no drugs or liqueurs that stimulate long-term thinking. Good long-term thinking requires a Socrates, an Aristotle, a good teacher, the Son of God and the Holy Spirit who ask penetrating questions.

Chapter Six

Heart Meditations

May the words of my mouth and the meditation of my heart be pleasing in your sight, O LORD, my Rock and my Redeemer.—Psalm 19:14

The Biblical meaning of the words "meditation" and "heart," as in the phrase "meditation of my heart" face cultural and kinetic misunderstandings. Heart brings into mind a cardiovascular chamber. We hand out candy hearts on Valentine's Day and associate love with a rapid heart beat and less about life's real center, the heart of our consciousness, the human brain.

Meditation seems mystical and Eastern. The Transcendental Meditation of the 1960's gave its practitioners a tranquility experience. It was not that special. Others listened to Classical music or sat on a folding chair placed among pines and maple trees. Zen meditation sought flashes of intuition by obstructing the mind's natural will to reason. Earth awaits for something tangible or meaningful from Zen.

Biblical and neurological meditation is more akin to the legal term "premeditation." Was the murder premeditated? Or, was the murder more like an animal act: instinctive, without any conscious reasoning? The legal system and the jury understand that you can't read or hear the heart of the accused. Yet twelve men and women consider exterior actions. The suspect downloaded articles on how to get away with murder. He purchased poison, a shovel, duck tape, a super-size plastic bag and a one-way ticket to Rio the day before. The jury sits in the jury box quietly listening but their hearts are meditating and speaking, "I know what you did. I know what you were thinking." The circumstantial and compelling evidence convict the defendant of meditating and acting a capital crime. What we meditate upon we often act. What we think stimulates our entire bodies. Our heart races, we get goose bumps, our faces turn read, our muscles twitch to musical rhythms. We run, dance or get sick. We kill.

When I worked on my books on the Chinese Christian leader Watchman Nee (1903-1972) I was surprised to find that he mentions so little about the heart. He had spent much time on church authority and interpreting "spirit, soul and body," but neglected the heart of human character, the mind. He's not the only Christian writer/preacher to neglect the workings of the heart. After decades of reading and listening to thousands of sermons, I have have concluded that American Christianity thinks of the heart in only two ways: God hardening pharaoh's heart and Jesus getting into my heart.

What exactly happened to Pharaoh's heart? There are only two possible meanings, neither is specifically evil. To "harden" means to strengthen. In the Hebrew Old Testament David strengthened his resolve to help his friend Jonathan. The Hebrew uses the same phrase "hardened heart." But it may also mean hardened our heart's wall to entertain a different idea. That idea is morally neutral. My heart is hardened about wife-beating and murder; won't do it. But I have an open heart whenever there is compelling evidence that the defendant committed assault or murder.

What does it mean when we say Jesus came into my heart? If Jesus comes into my heart and he is God, don't our bodies become a temple where God speaks and the law is stored? As the body of Christ, the church is also the temple. If we can speak of the church's inner sanctuary, then surely it is the heart, the center of our thoughts. Christ's there making our hearts

His home. We still have free will. We can ignore Him but He is there. We can let the Holy Spirit cleanse the temple or hope that the Spirit will leave or stay quiet.

But what thoughts and images do we mediate on? There's so much going on in physical World. How do we focus on what is important? "Focus, focus on one thing, like a laser beam," one talk show host tells a scattered-brained caller. "What's the one point you want to make?"

My brain consists of neurons that are not exactly connected. My brain cells have gaps, called synapses, that separate themselves from their neighbors. That's a good thing. Our brains have to limit the glory of the outside world. Creation is just too intense for mortal memories to handle the information coming from World. The synapses act as gate-keepers and surge protectors to keep down the volume. By choosing to focus our eyes, noses and ears on what is important we can take control on our neural chemicals. The choice give us better recall on what is memorable. But the Holy Ghost is in the house, he's pushing us to see what is good. We can control synap choices.

I make my mind happier by reading good books, looking at virtuous paintings and pictures and not letting the TV producers and advertisers decide

What do you meditate on?

By my desk is a picture of General Dwight D. Eisenhower mingling with paratroopers of the 502 Parachute Infantry Battalion on June 5th, 1944. They are preparing for D-Day invasion of France. Everyone there knows that many will die. I am reminded how much the general hated war and yet sacrifices have to be made in a crusade for peace and Freedom. Some will die so that good men might life. On the other wall is a framed poster entitled "Autumn Leaves of New England." On another wall is a picture of my twin sister and I. We are eleven years old.

I watch a few movies over and over again; films like *Trip to Bountiful, Awakenings, Isaac Stern in China, Hamlet* (1990), *Shawshank Redemption, To End All Wars, Apollo 13, Shadowlands and* Armand Nicholi's *The Question of God.*

There are also films directed by Alfred Hitchcock and John Ford. Yet I remember only nine at any one time.

In my college days some of us listened to Beatles record albums backwards, listening for secret messages that Paul McCartney or God was dead. A waste to time. Now I listen carefully for the sublime, shift of notes in Vivaldi, Gershwin, Rogers and Hammerstein, Bach and Mendelssohn, and vocals given by such notables as Nat King Cole, Perry Como, John McDermott, Paul Potts, Jon Vickers, Sumi Jo and Gladys Knight. Thank God for so many great masters of pop, jazz, ethnic sounds, Baroque and classical. Today I went outside tuned in on an hour of backyard arboreal and aviary melodies. The concert was interrupted by a twin-engine prop descending to the local airport. The leaves fall, the birds sang. The concert ended in a gentle fly-by. Thanks be to God for the amazing variety of music.

Be Careful

Be careful. The heart and the body are integrated. A healthy mind needs a healthy body. Christianity under the influence of Platonism tries to separate body from soul. Early European artists and physicians dissected bodies to find the seat or chamber of the soul. Some Christian writers spent much effort to separate and delineate the Biblical words into body, soul and spirit. The problem with that approach is that it minimizes the importance of the empty tomb. Consciousness and our self-identity are so integrated with the body that Paul had to reassure Christians that we get a temporary body/tent until the new Heaven and Earth is created. While our self-consciousness is a shadow or image of God, it also has the limitations of a physical body. Don't get drunk, don't take mind-altering drugs. Coffee awakens but does not alter perception.

Be careful. Some scientists and some religious groups have forgotten what they learned in English class about similes and metaphors. While the Bible does talk of the "hand of God" ten times the Bible is not teaching God is a 'Superman' floating around the cosmos like a Greek and Roman God. Scientists preach and attack a god in our image. It's a "straw man." It is an informal fallacy of substituting the traditional incorporable image of God for that proposed by nontraditional religious groups. It's the very same fallacy that motivates atheistic scientists to accept the Genesis of the the fundamentalist creation science of the nineteenth century as traditional Christianity.

Be careful. The words of our mouth are not always the words in our hearts. Vulnerable women and children have to be especially wise. Every bar, nearly every college campus and too many churches have wolves and serpents. The wolves draw victims away from public webs to a private ones. Before the police can be called, they need the protection and vigilance provided by the older and the wiser. They also need to keep sober introspection:

> Wait a minute. This is stupid. I met this man for ten minutes in a bar and he's offering to take me for a ride. I don't know his parents. I don't know his friends. I don't even know where he lives.

There's nothing more ridiculous and absurd as a girl falling in love with a man in prison "falsely convicted" of rape or criminal violence. If he is really innocent let the criminologists prove it before making romantic commitments. Since the 1960's American culture has endorsed "groovy" feelings devoid of reason and introspection. They have put down their swords; the wolves are waiting.

Be careful. Spoken words and clothes are worn on the outside. They don't always reveal the heart. Cultures or sub-cultures untrained in introspection and heart meditations judge people by stage performances, "fabulous clothes" and skin color. We are not surprised when Hollywood and sports pop stars have irregular personal lives. Wearing Armani sunglasses, clothes by Oleg Cassini, Herbert James Tafflin de Givenchy, Christian Dior or even Saffron robes; reveal more what you want people to think, less of who you really are. And what of the guy whose trousers are hanging below his butt crack? Does he want to be cool, to learn from the wise or is he afraid of them? The clothes don't tell.

Be careful. Words can be a stage performance. Words can be an act. Some Southern racists who publicly warned about miscegenation were rapists, had black mistresses, or both. Since the days of Charles G. Finney preaching has become more theater. Some mega church messages and TV preaching consist of 'secrets' drawn out of a few Biblical words and spoken with a so-called "anointed voice." The hair, the wardrobe are of course "fabulous." The performance is more acting than substance. When the real secrets of the ministry are revealed, shame, not glory, fall upon God's word. In the film *Osama* (2003) director Siddiq Barmak warns us that the pious spiritual garb of mullahs may hide carnal intent. I have listened and read many of the instructions of the Dalai Lama. He's preaching is not so much Tibetan as it is Buddhism mingled with the discredited pop psychobabble I heard in the 1970's. It's just packaged in a different way.

When the police investigate 'persons of interest' we don't want police to judge by the cut of their threads or the color of their skin. Good police work looks for evidence of actions and evidence of the heart. God is the best judge because he sees the heart. We can't. But police, with a court order, can seize high tech extensions of our heart: the computer hard drive . If forensic technicians discover a lot of computer time searching for information about getting away with murder and corroborating emails to another 'person of interest' the police are reading a criminal heart. When God searches the images of hearts will he find images of Himself and the bride and bridegroom? Have the eyes of your heart become fixed upon Christ who died for us, or upon the love of power and money?

Clothes should change our feelings, not our neighbor's. The cop wears an American flag to remind him that he serves law, flag, and Constitution. I put on a RAF pilot's cap and remember the sacrifice of British and American servicemen in defense of freedom. I don't pretend to be a pilot. I raise my cap high to soldiers, veterans, and the God who gives us true freedom. Jews wear phylacteries, verses of Scripture worn on the forehead and arm, to remind themselves to think (forehead) and act (arm) according to the Torah, the five books of Moses. When I put on creased trousers; long-sleeve dress shirt, matching tie; and polished shoes I am more organized. I also like wearing cardigan sweaters. My students speculated that I was trying to be like children's television superstar Mr. Rogers. Did I wear that kind of sweater because I want "to be your neighbor"? Or, perhaps I am living in the 'Land of Make Believe'? Not really. I wear cardigan sweaters for the same two reasons that Mr. Rogers did: to keep warm and it was the style worn by the greatest generation. They defeated tyranny, landed men on the moon and discovered the polio vaccine. They thought that being at home with the wife and kids was just fine. I want to be like them. I also want to be your neighbor by talking and listening.

Be careful There are warnings in Scripture about moral heart disease that poses a health threat to others. In Psalm 5:8 David speaks of his enemies. It fits some of our enemies: "Not a word from their mouth can be trusted; their heart is filled with destruction. Their throat is an open grave; with their tongue they speak deceit."(NIV) The most common heart disease is pride in oneself. We are all subject to this disease. It's a self-deception. In Hosea, God reminds us that there is no Savior but Him. "When I fed them, they were satisfied; when they were satisfied, they became proud; then they forgot me." (Hos. 13:6 NIV) Remember Mary's poem? "He [God] hath shown strength with his arm; he hath scattered the proud in the imagination of their hearts." (Lk 1:51 KJV)

Materialists think thought is purely biochemical and consciousness, an illusion. Recently I heard a lecture by such a scientist. Ironically he still permitted himself the luxury of first person pronouns. He introduced nearly every one of his opinions with "I think" instead of "my brain thinks" or "it thinks." His lectures betrayed his own disposition to an integrated dualism that most of us experience. We can deceive ourselves and others. God can't deceive Himself.

Chapter 7

The Heart of Language

Creative speaking/writing is no accident. Mathematical theoreticians have dismissed the myth that given enough monkeys and enough time one monkey will type a Shakespearean play. That is . . "not to be." If you role dice a few thousand times it is very likely you will get 'lucky sevens' four or five times in a row. But what are the chances that a chimp will accidentally type "I love you"? The keyboard has 50 keys. The monkey has to hit in the right sequence of ten keys. His chances then are one in 50^{10}, one chance in 97,656,250,000,000,000 every time the monkey hits ten keys. We can increase the chances by raising more monkeys. We will also need the earth's human population manufacturing keyboards and cleaning keyboards (When chimpanzees get excited it's not coffee they spill on keyboards.).

Each year thousands of books are written and published in the United States alone. The earth is full of languages. Our brains are hot wired for grammar. After a year of life infant vocal chords are activated for talking. Between three and four years a child's language surpasses the imitative abilities of the best trained primates. By the age four, children have already made an enormous and strategic leap in thought and language. They can listen to their thinking inside. They start thinking about thinking and asking "Why?" "Where did I come from?" The secondary conscious has awakened. They can freely call up images from the past without external stimuli. The buds of speech have blossomed to forms the seeds of new ideas and sentences. They build new sentences and wonder about the stars. They wonder where they came from and what happened to Grandpa. They have an operating secondary consciousness; they have a heart. They can talk to themselves without moving their lips.

The miracle happens in early childhood. "We have lift-off!" We escaped the bonds of animal thinking and can search the stars. We can search for Santa and the reindeer. We can search for the real star of Bethlehem.

In college I had a philosophy teacher who suggested that Jesus is God's self-awareness not a separate god. In our brains we talk and another self listens. A third self, my animation, has neural connections touching nearly every muscle and skin cell. It enables my skin to bubble up in goose bumps and allows my fingers to glide along the computer keyboard nearly detached from my other thought processes. It is only when I am first learning to type that I make conscious effort to find where the "e" key is. The twenty-five mile drive from my house to Atlanta's airport is familiar territory. Because it is, I can easily focus my attention on self-talk, old memories, an audio book, or a talk show conversation. At night and in unfamiliar travels I turn off the radio and focus on signs and landmarks.

Does God talk to himself? We can, by logic, eliminate from God's consciousness the idea that he says something like:

"Avocados: I should have made the seeds smaller."

"I'm tired of playing with dinosaurs. I'll just throw this big rock at them and make furry creatures."

"I'll think I'll make my Ken and Barbie dolls alive and put them in a garden."

We all laugh at a God in the image of George Burns in the film *Oh, God* (1977). Yet this kind of talking god persists in the imagination of non Western religions and in the imagination of atheists. It was the logic of Athens and Jerusalem, of Aristotle and Elijah, that filed the gods of Greece and Rome into the mythology section of the public library. It's prejudice to put all religions there.

    The Scriptures make the connection that self-talking is in the image of God. In Genesis 1:25 God speaks to Himself. It's not the first time. God talks to that part of his personal character that was there before Abraham was. Jesus goes to a solitary place to talk to his Father. He preaches "Before Abraham was, I am". Before the first Christian, before the first Jew asks God to reshape their lives, "the Spirit of God was hovering over the face of the deep." There's a voice. There's God there talking to Himself. There is also a Spirit, the Holy Spirit, that creates and inspires the prophets. Does God talk to the Spirit in His heart or does he talk to another aspect of Himself? Here Jews and Christians are free to disagree.

The "I" Conference.

Some years ago I read Noam Chomsky's work on the mind's generative grammar. There's much truth in what he says. Our brain is neurologically designed to create language within certain predefined (predestined) patterns. Yet there is something missing in his essay. The broad expanse of languages, dialects, stylistic variations and writing speaking/creativity can not be explained by just grammatical neurons. We create new sentences and new languages by listening and talking to others and especially to ourselves. Like many scientific explanations of the mind, its place, its art and beauty, are ignored or remain unseen to behaviorists and neurologists alike. It is an undiscovered country. Its a place that we visit often and we find comfort.

Just think about it, meditate for a moment. Who do we talk to most? Our parents? Our children? Our spouse? Or, ourselves? Within our heads we have brainstorms. Outwardly, scientists, managers, engineers, students of the Bible, even the president's cabinet get together to brainstorm. Out of the discussion comes new ideas. We all do it inwardly. When I shave in the morning, when I drive to work I have a brainstorm conference with myself (A good night sleep and a cup of coffee keeps the conversation lively.). Some of the things I read the night before turn into something original. My mind had deconstructed a number of Lego ideas built by others and set up a new set of mental images. I sit down and write the thoughts into a file on my laptop. As I type each word, I listen to the same words narrated by the "I" voice in my heart. In the evening I check and edit what I wrote. I check for grammatical and typing errors and for vanity.

The Bible identifies thinking as speech in the heart. There is, for example, a difference between speaking a prayer and "praying in my heart" (Genesis 24:45), reading scripture and reading with the heart. They are prayer books used in the worship services of a number of Christian denominations. Many of them are masterpieces of words. But the familiarity of the words and its recitation can become like well traveled highways.

We can say them or hear them and yet have our minds on something else. I remember attending an interdenominational worship service. One of the clergyman got all the way through reading a footnote as "the word of the Lord" before he realized his mistake. His heart was on other things.

The Greek and Hebrew words for heart appear more often in Scripture than we read. Translations of the Bible don't always translate "heart" consistently. It is not a matter of deception. Unlike the English language and modern culture the Bible uses the heart infrequently for a physical organ (Psalm 38:10). Translators can faithfully substitute words like "thought" and "thinking."

"What were you thinking?" is a expression common to those who work or live with adolescents. The reply might be, "Nothing." This is not true. In most, if not all cases, adolescent accidents are about meditating on the wrong subject at the wrong time. Bad college students meditate on other things and often blame the lecturer. Lecturer incompetency may or may not be the case. Often the student's desire for sleep, painful meditations on hangovers, or the trinity of "sex, drugs and rock'n'roll" hinders learning. Sadly, some teachers lower the bar of excellence to earn tenure for themselves and tuition money for the college.

Jesus challenged his disciples with ponderous questions and sublime parables. In Luke 4:17, He opened the Isaiah scroll and helped us see the world and our times in a different way. But many of his disciples today don't meditate on the lilies of the field nor see image of Christ in the hungry. They chirp and bark out Scripture quotes and theological precepts without pondering and meditating inwardly what how to walk outside.

When Shakespeare wishes to show what a man is pondering in his heart he uses the soliloquy, a theatrical technique to reveal to the audience character, and character indecision and character change. Too often today's modern Christians, in tune with the electronic age, have thoughts more in mind with Shakespeare's Polonius than Scripture's Spirit inspired authors. In Shakespeare's *Hamlet. Polonius* was a man wise in his own eyes and full of hand-me-down cliches devoid of personal reflection. His wisdom is all staged; it does not come from the heart. In Act 3 Scene 2, Polonius tells Hamlet that he "was accounted a good actor." When asked for details Polonoius says that he played Julius Caesar. There is a double meaning to this. The play "Julius Caesar" may have been performed just before "Hamlet." The same actor may have played Caesar and Polonius. Both characters are superficial. They never take things to heart as Hamlet does.

God gives us the art of words that He has. God gives hearts to all, not just Jews and Christians. Not all hearts enjoy the light of God's life, or love wisdom. They close the clapboards to keep the light out. God's love, justice and mercy are not welcome They don't meditate and use reason. Reason, Aristotle considered the most divine part of our natures. Yet all of us have the shadow/image of God.

From about the age of three till the hour of our death we display the creative image of God. When my daughter Jennifer was just three years old she started creating stories of monsters. She told me that the bushes help protect the good monsters from the bad ones. My other daughter Rebecca typed a wondrous word picture on my computer screen of a girl watching the moon from her bedroom window. It was in the same lyrical style of children's books. The picture was unique and quite visible to me. I was amazed at the carving skill of my great grandfather William Roberts. He carved a grandfather clock cherished by my grand aunt Ruth. He carved lion's paws as its feet and Corinthian columns along its casing. According to family tradition, which I can't confirm, he carved the Oak Room of the Copley Plaza Hotel in Boston. Before the first board was cut, before the first wood shaving fell to the floor he created the clock and the Oak Room in his mind

And what of my own skills? I wish I had learned the violin, but my mother said, "You can have violin lessons or lunch. I can't afford both." The library card was free and paperback books cheap. Fortunately there will be time enough in heaven to learn to slide the bow, to sing without a stuffy nose and to sit and share words with old friends and the likes of Malcolm Muggeridge, Blaise Pascal, and Boris Pasternak.

Pocket Books

Every time I read a book, even a comic book, I am astonished at the extraordinary we share with God. When I was young I filled my mind with images from books. I left my house on a tree-lined street in Dedham, Massachusetts, walked a short distance and entered a rain forest. Timbers supported a flat roof and the ceiling fans. Every wood case niche housed leaves bound and preserved, stitched and stapled into books and magazines. As a child, created in God's image, I gazed upon each leave whose alphanumeric veins were food for the heart. It was a library and I had a library card. I search the shelves. I found good books. I Read them. If my friends and three sisters were too busy to speak Ray Bradbury, or Bruce Catton was there to tell a story. Written words communicate just as well as moving lips.

According to one family tradition I was named after the actor Dana Andrews (1909-1992)]. That may be true. I remember that TV and movie magazines were all the home schooling I received. My Mom was somewhat of an expert on the subject of Debbie Reynolds, Eddie Fisher; Elizabeth Taylor and Burt Reynolds. After school there was "Queen for a Day." Five O'clock was the Mickey Mouse Club. Weekends were reserved for Steve Allen and Ed Sullivan. The closest thing to educational TV came from reruns of "Victory at Sea." But with books I was with the Lost Battalion, flying over Germany in a Lancaster bomber and looking for Japanese snipers on Guadalcanal.

I started hanging around with a gang. We were three or four guys who usually carried pocketbooks to school. Its not what you think. Back in the fifties and early sixties a pocketbook was a soft cover book, small and portable enough to fit in a trouser back pocket. I still have the copy of my first paperback, *Galaxies Like Grains of Sand* by Brian Aldriss (1960). It was a chronicle of the future (I can still envision the robots celebrating the death of what they thought was the last man on earth.). I saw on TV films *The Day the Earth Stood Still* and *Forbidden Planet*. But we wanted more stories and more choices. My friends and I began to wonder if there were flying saucers. The best TV and books, in our minds, were anthologies of unexplained phenomena and science fiction "what ifs." We read Frank Edwards' *Stranger than Science* and Frank Scully's *Flying Saucers are Real*. We were young; we read adult nonsense. My choice of books was not rocket science. But science classes and the good intentions of reading teachers changed all that. Just thirteen I heard the "Song of Hiawatha" and "Under a Chestnut Tree" spoken as if each word was delivered by a resurrected dead poet. A year later I discovered Reader's Digest and the joy of good, clean laughter. I was reading and watching.

When Kennedy was shot I was reading *The Day Lincoln was Shot* by Jim Bishop, I started reading about presidential assassinations. When the Warren Commission came out I read an abridged edition and Gerald Ford's biography of Lee Harvey Oswald. When I started hearing conspiracy theories on radio talk shows I thought back to all the speculation and superficial flying saucer evidence I had read. I didn't read books that used the word "suppose" and "perhaps" to speculate on a conspiracy and then portray speculation as evidence.

A trip away from home often meant a walk to Oakdale Square. The Episcopal and Methodist Churches gave the square a mild pastoral sanctity. Shoe repair and barber shops, a market, candy store, drug store and local branch of the Dedham Public Library made my neighborhood just as appealing as Frank Capra's Bedford Falls. At least once a month I'd go down to the drug store and sip on an ice cream frappe at the soda fountain. I'd fill a thirst for truth and adventure by spinning the paperback rack. I met Ellery Queen, Ian Fleming and 007.

From paperbacks I learned that my town was more Amish than the rest of America. In Dedham I never saw young girls in cocktail dresses with plunging necklines, approachable smiles

Seeing the Unseen

and mink wraps. But they were there . . . on the covers of Mickey Spillane and Earl Stanley Gardner.

Still my sanctuary was the library rain forest. I remember its store front image befitting for the Eisenhower era or even a decade earlier. In my heart I can still walk inside the two public rooms lined with dust-jacketed hard back volumes. The main room resonated with the noise of children searching "age appropriate" collections, librarian inquiries, the pounding of rubber stamps dating loan stickers inside the covers of each volume. There were brief moments of gossip among Oakdale's neighbors. Just to the right of the librarian's desk was my corner, "Young adult non-fiction." The other room was the silent reading room. There we were supposed to silently sit and read, or do homework on the hard wood conference table.

The only long fiction I ever remember taking out of that library was a young adult abridgment of *The Odyssey* and a well-footnoted, complete translation of *The Iliad*. Since that time I have come to enjoy many fine novels. Yet today I still fight a conscious, irrational skepticism about fiction. It takes me a month to read the first fifty pages and the next five days to read the next three hundred. It's a nonsense tick.

Great fiction can tell us more about humanity than the psychobabble texts starting with Freud and continuing with Deepak Chopra, Wayne Dyer and the Dali Lama. Great novelists sold their wisdom stories for daily bread and shelter. Their honor often came posthumously. Solzhenitsyn, Tolstoy and Dostoevsky and the writing prophets understand us more than today's psycho-gnostics. England's metaphysical poets, Russian novelists and China's New Realism post-revolutionary writers and film directors understood suffering humanity more than today's lounge wizards of guilt-free narcissism. But it is the latter, pop writers that gain fame on Oprah . . . even worship.

In the time between I read my first adult book to the present, the world has witnessed jet travel; men on the moon; deep sea, Titanic discoveries; CAT scans and personal computers. Yet the greatest miracle is natural: the gift of language, words, words and more words. Without them there is no science. There is no history, no poetry and no moral accountability.

I particularly enjoy the poetry and prose of William Saroyan. During World War II he wrote *The Human Comedy* first as a film script and then as a novel. It's a story about why our civilization fights. We need to read it today. Today the United States has nearly three times the population. We protest the death of a dozen in combat. Back then there were some weeks when newspapers and telegraph offices reported more than a 1,000 combat deaths. It was a "Crusade" as General Eisenhower called it, a crusade to defeat evil. Saroyan dramatizes the "good" in the fictional town of Ithaca, California, in one family, in men on a troop train, in a telegraph office, a classroom and in the public library. Two friends, the young boy Ulysses and his unlearned friend Lionel, visit the town library. Neither one can read. Yet the older Lionel teaches by word and action that he understands the holiness of words.

> "This is the pubalic liberry, Ulysses," he said. "Books all over the place." He looked at the print of the book with a kind of reverence, whispering to himself as if he were trying to read. Then he shook his head. "You can't know what a book says, Ulysses, unless you can read, and I can't read," he said.
>
> He closed the book slowly, put it back in its place, and together the two friends tiptoed out of the library. Outside, Ulysses kicked up his heel because he felt good, and because it seemed he had learned something new.[5]

The Greatest Generation fought for words and public libraries. It was a time when books were burned in Berlin and elsewhere. In some cultures today owning a Bible and books on freedom and democratic ideals is a crime subject to burning and even beheading. While there are books that encourage evil, a virtuous individual understands that he has to be skeptical. He has a responsibility ask questions, "Is this edifying? Will this build character and build society?

"Any jackass can kick down down an old barn. But it takes a carpenter to build one." It's an old New England proverb. The carpenter is skilled. He knows his stuff. It takes more skill to create an idea than to criticize.

We live in an age predicted by science fiction writer and technology critic Ray Bradbury. In his 1951 novel *Fahrenheit 451* warns of a future America where flat-screened TVs and electronic media have replaced books. Trivia or "factoids" have replaced knowledge. Hedonism has replaced passion and virtue.

In 1964 my tastes changed it was though someone was inside my mind, changing my tastes in words and images. I can't say I always listened to God's advice, but I began to search the library stacks, used bookstores, record shops and art galleries for "whatever is true, whatever is noble, whatever is right, whatever is pure, whatever is lovely, whatever is admirable—if anything is excellent or praiseworthy" (Philippians 4:8).

Students today do more watching than reading. They have become so unskilled at reading that they their hearts fall to plagiarism. In some colleges it's so bad that teachers are instructed to look away.

The Heart as Language Laboratory

God give us hearts as laboratories to create music, words and ideas. Our language skills are boosted by our ability to hold visual and audio memories in an area that philosopher Karl Popper calls World 2.[6]

> *World 1* is the "physical" world. In our day-to-day lives. It's the office, the interstate highway, our home, the diner where I get eggs sunny-side, buttered toast and a good cup of Java.

> *World 2* is our consciousness, the world of mental phenomena, our decision maker. It is the home of our self-talk. In the Bible it is called the heart.

> World 3 is the world of accumulated knowledge, sense and nonsense, in books, culture and ideas.

The worlds interact. World 2 is where minds constantly gather information from Worlds 1 and 3. World 2 creates mental memories, ideas and can contribute to World 3. .When the worlds are healthy they don't don't collide. There is synchrony. Synchrony is the fulfillment of America's pursuit of happiness and the western tradition. Synchrony is peace, shalom.

Healthy minds have the ability to fantasize and create worlds that they know are not real. Schizophrenics are not sure what is real and what is imagined. The healthy know that Narnia and Middle Earth are full of truth and yet fictional. The tales are less related to the physical world than what's in our homes and neighborhood. Yet the fantasy novels of C. S. Lewis and J. R. R. Tolkien and the plays of William Shakespeare tell us much about ourselves. Great novelists, poets and playwrights put a lot of thought and insight into words. They can tell us more about life than so-called objective news reporting or what "science says." You can learn more psychology from the Bible and Shakespeare than you can learn from Freud and

Seeing the Unseen

Magnetic Resonate Imaging (MRI). When we are poor in spirit, living in broken homes, or pursue any goal it is in the heart's imaginations that hope buds and blooms. We dream a dream and then we seek to fulfill it.

Wise minds acknowledge the insights of literature, the facts of science and good reporting. They realize that there is no such thing as entirely objective news. Editors decide what goes to print and what doesn't. The best we can hope for is an editor who asks his staff important questions: Has the seven minute video report or the 800 word article acknowledged all the data? How much of this is fact? How much spurious speculation?

World 3 is the world of culture, past recollections and ideas printed on paper. Culture is painted on walls and canvasses, and monuments of cloth, wood, stone and gold. Within the past two centuries it has moved further away from constitutional reason and debate to flash video images.

Good luck charms and astrology are still part of World 3. They may infect World 2. They are of no value living in World 1.

Today's pop culture minimizes the importance of reason and rationality. Modern media interprets the physical world as real and objective; the mental world as subjective and unreal. But as philosopher Karl Popper has pointed out the scientific/mathematical community is mistaken. Science and math have to go through the mind. Once an idea, even a simple addition problem, is in our heads it competes with other ideas and images. It is subjective because our minds make judgments about its importance and how much time it takes up in our conscious thoughts. Only extreme autistic savants think the number of cracks on the sidewalk and the matches in the matchbox sharing equal time with questions fit for eternity. With reason we separate the important from the unimportant, our needs from our wants, the good and the bad, and the ugly. Reason arises in the meditations of our hearts.

I meditate about political issues. I have become cautious about health care promises. There are often unforeseen consequences and trade offs. Many political decisions fail, especially the grand ones. Yesterday I watched the evening news and noticed that all of the sponsors were pharmaceutical companies. Today I watched the morning news. Most of the ads were from the health care industry, selling drugs whose effectiveness are often overrated. There was an ad from a medical malpractice law firm. The news is not objective. The news staff and editors are not intentionally lying but they may have more a bias to thank their financial backers. They may see a health care emergency greater than there really is. They can't show all the news. Simple ideas like "health care crisis" makes more money and quicker to swallow than complicated ideas like unnecessary pharmaceutical copyright extensions, spurious medical tests and lawsuits. Since my high school days these problems have raised the cost of medicine. We are told that spending federal and municipal funds to subsidize costs are necessary.

In America much reasoning is based upon quantity than quality. Why are American medicals costs so high? As I write this book, advocates of public health care see it as a code three emergency. The cure is 1500 pages of legislation. Are they right? How did we get into this mess so quickly. It is hard to tell by commercial TV. Does the pharmaceutical-media connection directly or indirectly shade the reporting? I ask myself, "Has the virtues of medical research and capitalism turned into a destructive tax burden and greed?" Medicine is good, but bankrupting a nation is not.

In 2007, I had taken part in a jury analysis of a lawsuit against the nursing staff at local hospital that resulted in death. The jury did make the right decision. The nurses had neglected their responsibilities. The family was awarded $5,000,000. One prospective juror thought $30,000,000 would fit the crime. I thought no more than two. The nurses didn't pay. Do jurors ever wonder who really pays the lawsuit awards? The number of frivolous or costly lawsuits in the state of Georgia alone places a great burden on health insurance costs. The law offices are the biggest winner. If TV new reporters, paid by pharmaceutical and law firm advertisements, acted like judges they would have to step down from reporting for personal bias.

Besides decision making, the heart creates and speaks new ideas, to form new ways of telling stories, even "the old old story of Jesus and His love." A liberal arts education adds depth and content. The original intent of liberal arts was to refine our understanding of the world with words, music and art. The educated author mulls over his choice of words and the scenes he creates. The educated reader responds by mulling over the same words and scenes. The best musicians and composers are well trained in the history and language of music as they daily exercise the keys and the strings. Painters study. They search their heads for a technique and a style to fit the subject. The more styles and techniques the art students master the better the visual message. Education and meditation accomplish great things.

When Mendelssohn composed the "Wedding March" for "Shakespeare's *A Midsummer Night's Dream* his mind most surely remembered and meditated on Johann Sebastian Bach's marriage melody in the *St. Matthew Passion.* And, Bach had reminisced on a wedding tune composed by a forgotten French troubadour.

Music adds tone, pacing and texture to the language of life, poetry and the camera's eye. I have loved violin music since childhood. In college I bought a collection of classical recordings by the Russian violinist David Oistrakh (1908-1974). I have video's of violinist Isaac Stern playing in Israel (1967) and in China (1979). I have half a dozen DVD's of the violin masters. A musical piece played on the same instrument, with the same arraignment still conveys a voice unique to every violinist. I have purchased or borrowed a number of sound recordings of my favorite violin masterpiece, Felix Mendelssohn's Violin Concerto in E Minor(1844). It seems to capture all the joyous emotions that Christians can have (He may have been inspired by an infatuation and admiration for Swedish soprano Jenny Lind.). I have listened to the piece performed by David Oistrakh, Isaac Stern, Sarah Chang, Chen Mei, Sarah Chang, Yehudi Menuihin, Annie Sophie Mutter and Jascha Heifetz. Some recordings are aged and lack fidelity. Some fortunate artists

Seeing the Unseen

played a Stradivarius or a Guarnerius violin. They play the same concerto yet the voice is different. Master musicians transform the violin to express their own accent and passion. The violin becomes their voice and local dialect. How do they do it? They practice and meditate meaning into each note. It's as the idiom says, "they put their heart and soul into it." It's like the unique tone and passion that each actor renders Shakespeare's "To be or Not to be."

Music adds immeasurably to visual images. In 1975 I saw the film *Jaws*. If music director John Williams had played Mendelssohn's *Wedding March from Midsummer Night's Dream* instead of his own ominous accelerating shark theme we'd have laughter instead of fear. The film would be labeled black humor instead of a thriller.

Music does the same to the written word of God. Open the Bible right in the middle and what do you read? The Book of Psalms is great poetry intended to be a great musical. This musical is not about a high school infatuation. Its melodies sing of a full range of divine and human experiences. It's a musical comedy and a tragedy. Like Shakespeare's plays, each psalm is either a comical tragedy or a tragic comedy.

The Bible inspires us to connect melodies with prayer and worship. When I read the Gospels I sometimes hear music. For three hundred years the children of Israel were without the prophet's direction. I listen to myself reading the first three chapters of the Gospel of Luke. I close my eyes and think of that silent time between the testaments. The prophetic silence was like the drought in Elijah's day. Then slowly God's word comes. Elijah's sees "a cloud as small as a man's hand." Shortly thereafter "the sky grew black with clouds, the wind rose, a heavy rain." (1Ki 18:45 NIV) As I read about John the Baptist and the coming of Christ I hear the sound of Vivaldi's "Winter Theme." Drip, drip goes the harpsichord; Simeon and Anna speak at the temple. The violins speed up the pace. Then there is an outpouring, a wall of sound. It is a great storm, it is a heavy rain. Vivaldi may have thought of a storm in Venice and possibly the raging storms in people's minds. It is also John the Baptist and the great coming of the Lord. Luke's words and the conclusion of Vivaldi's music become sublime metaphors for the totally wet, immersion of Holy Spirit administered by the Messiah.

I love passionate Christian music and reading different translations. If the music is not just imitating pop styles, religious and classical music conveys worship even if it is in an unknown tongue. I love Bach's German, Handel's English, Chinese, Korean, Tamil, Spanish and Italian spirituals. The Bible has been translated into thousands of languages. Muslims believe that the Qur'an can only be written in the original Arabic. Translations are merely commentaries. Yet Jews and Christians take very seriously the work of translation. The Bible and the Holy Spirit translates God's ways into the life of all nations

Creativity comes from the heart. Whether it is creating new sentences, a new song, a work of art or a scientific discovery it's crafted in the heart. I love painting. There is something quite akin to the the work of God in creation and that of the painter. The Bible speaks of God's creating as a shaping and separating the earth and its waters. Today's modern painters get their colors out of tubes. But artists of the Renaissance saw the paint-making as the preparation of a sacrament. They recreated the primordial dust of the earth (ground rock) and mixed it with liquid to create water colors, oils and tempera (egg). They mixed the two essences with the care, love of art and intuitive sense of proportion shared by another group of artists. Today's culinary masters of Italian homes make "the sauce" without the use of measure spoons. As one Sicilian-American matron explained, "It's in the eyes, the fingers, the tongue." I can't say for sure whether the early European artists tasted their concoctions, but they certainly used the other senses. They held paint brushes in a way, a far different way than the Chinese 'maobi' artists. The brush is like the bowstring as of violin or the tone arm of phonograph. The brush is held in the hand for control and to feel texture. The heart of the painters pours forth speech, telling himself what perspective to make, what shade and color and whether to see it as "good" or "bad."

Until the 19th century painters generally saw their arts as a cooperation of the artists God-given skills, the divine laws that govern chemistry/alchemy, and the visual illusion within the mind of the viewers. With care the layers of paint created a two-dimensional world, seen as three. In their hearts they meditated on God's word and their own work. Like the six days of creation, dry land, seas, plants and animals and faces formed out of the dust and waters of the earth. The early Dutch Master Jan van Eyck (1395-1441) signed his work with "als ich kan," "as I am able to." The Netherlander community understood. The artists is able by the grace of God. Artists sometimes saw themselves as Christ-like. The priest reenacts Christ's breaking of the bread. The artist reenacts Christ's work of creating a new man and foreshadows the creation of the new heaven and earth. Albrecht Durer (1471-1528) painted a self-portrait of himself as Jesus Christ. He was not that mad, nor that vain. Like the actor in a passion play he acts like Christ on the world's stage. We are surely not mad to call ourselves Christians, little Christ's.

Out of the mind's heart, something we share with God alone, comes all the great ideas, the new inventions, most changes in character. It is also the chamber of divine inspiration.

The Bible best defines it in Genesis and in Psalm 19:14:

May the words of my mouth
    and
        the meditation of my heart be pleasing in your sight,
            O LORD, my Rock and my Redeemer.

Yet, there is a warning within this verse. The creative laboratory of the heart can also serve as a den of deception. Because we have an outer voice and an inner voices we can deceive and hide our true intentions. Like the fictional laboratory of Dr. Frankenstein, the laboratory of the heart can create a monster too. Every year we learn of pastors who serve their passion for women or greed while outwardly making exalted claims of a special anointing. Celebrities promote and fail to think with

Seeing the Unseen

hearts about buying monster SUV's and flying around in private carbon-based fuel guzzlers. We are so enamored by anti-war pop stars and neglect to ask how much their drug lifestyle fuels Mexico's deadly drug violence.

Genesis explains why there are deceptive hearts. What the senses take in are not all clear affirmations of God's goodness. We now live in a good world God created where the peaceful lamb as well as the fearful symmetry of the tiger thrive. In this world the lion does not lay down with the lamb. The tiger is not morally responsible for killing to feed her cubs. It is an unconscious instinct. Like the Garden of Eden God is enough absent from the land so that we can freely choose to be lambs, or tigers and ravenous wolves. Jesus says, "Watch out for false prophets. They come to you in sheep's clothing, but inwardly they are ferocious wolves." (Matthew 7:15) He also tell us that until the harvest the wheat and worthless weeds seem pretty much alike (Mathew 13:24-30).

While creation is good we still live in the twilight zone of God's glory. Each earth day is "evening and morning." It is not like the noon days of the "the new heaven and earth"(Rev. 22:5).God's light is not everywhere directing and disciplining us. In the world there is the problem of evil and a loving God. According to Genesis' diagnosis the problem is in the very length of the created days.

I can't say how many times I have read Genesis one, nor how many times I have read it aloud. I have struggled to understand all its particulars, its sublime message. There's one particular oddity that commentaries rarely comment. There are six days of creation, but they're shorter, not longer, than a regular day. With the rise of Darwinian evolution and geology, American Christianity shifted away the traditional openness to wonder whether the texts speak of a regular earth day or a divine "single day can be a thousand years." Just how long is a day before the sun was created? They may not be the right question to ask. Throughout the Bible the question is not the length, but the light of the day.

At the very most it's six hours. They days are composed of "evening and morning." In graduate school I learned that the Hebrew word for "morning" is really a farmer's morning. The term for "evening" is really the twilight. Evening and morning are only six hours in the upper latitudes of the earth. In the land between the Tigris and Euphrates, dusk and dawn time is shorter. But is "evening and morning" about the length or the quality of the day?

In our consciousness time is as relative as relativity. There is a biological metronome in our heads. But sunlight quantity fluctuates with the seasons. Light bulbs and coffee resets our biological time. We measure our days by idle time, play and memorable events . We say, "Time flies when you're havin' fun." Or, "It's been a long day." The sense of time also changes the older we get. For a children, a year between Christmases is 10% of their lives; for me it's about 1.6 % of my life. Years feel shorter with each passing year.

I doubt that seventeen-year locusts have any sense of time at all. These cicadas spend seventeen years of their live as underground worms and then spend one frantic noisy week flying and trying to find a mate. So what about God's time? Earlier generations of Christians had a simple Biblical answer: "A single day is as a thousand years" (Psalm 90:4; 2 Peter 3:8). Even here, the word is not precise enough to mark it as a human millennium. It's "<u>as</u> a thousand years."

The Genesis days are marked by two terms; *evening and morning*. Many have consciously or unconsciously taken "evening and morning" as the literary idiom of synecdoche . . . a part representing the whole. The Bible does use synecdoche. This is clearly the case in the story of Adam. The story of Adam is the story of the whole of humanity based upon the story of one man and his one decision. It's true in the Lord's Prayer. When we pray for our daily bread we understand we are asking for foods to sustain us. It's a prayer just as much for a cup of coffee, pastrami sandwich and a kosher pickle as it is for a half a loaf of rye bread.

Are the six hours representing twenty-four? I don't think so. And, there are very good reasons to think not. Light and darkness in the Scripture represent two realms that overlap. The sun and moon are part of the physical universe. Light of "a different color" is the realm of God's activity; darkness its absence. On the first day there was no sun, moon or stars in the sky. Yet God separated the light from the darkness. Light exists because there is darkness.

When Jesus says, "I am the light of the world" we don't expect him to be our night light. Jesus spoke to the Jewish people, a nation who delighted in reading and in literature. Jesus' Jewish audience knew that he was not declaring that he glows in the dark. Instead Jesus declares that the light of God's Kingdom was there in Him. The world needs Him just as much at midnight as at midday.

The last book of the Bible helps us to understand the first book. In the very last chapter of the The Book of Revelation at verse 25, Christians read of a new Heaven and Earth. Its residents "will not need the light of a lamp or the light of the sun, for the Lord God will give them light." Jews and Christians understand the meaning. The angels on Heaven don't have to assure light-skin Norwegian believers, "Fear not! No sunburns here. No skin cancer. No premature aging. Your new, improved glorified bodies are immortal and spotless." You don't have to worry because the light of Heaven is not thermonuclear.

The "evening and morning" of creation days in Genesis are without the full light of the Lord. It is not entirely dark. There are signs of a new day or one passing away. Even though God's children are in His image, they walk in near darkness. There are enough signs to believe, or not to. If we search we will find. There are enough signs to find the way. Yet it's as though God has made the world into a game board, a game of clues. The solution to the game is not about who murdered Colonel Mustard with the candlestick in the library. The object of God's game of life is for us to collect or treasure clues into our hearts and make a decision: Will our life end as Shakespeare says "sans nothing" or with "flights of angels sing thee to they rest."

Chapter Eight

A Heart that Sees

~~~~

There are certain photos and images that stick in our imagination. Certain paintings have transcended generational tastes . . .

The painting is entitled *Afterglow.* It is by Maxfield Parrish. In the first half of the twentieth century Parrish was one of the top American painters. According to one author at least one of his paintings graced the walls of a fifth of the American homes. It is a twilight of a New England day. To capture its essence Parrish had to go out in the cold and stare. In 1927 no camera could capture that color. Parrish had to remember and meditate on the exact color tone of pink and blue to mix his paints. It is a snapshot, a brief moment in time.

It is a mystical moment. It draws attention to an unfulfilled, aesthetic longing. What do we long for? For the warmth of the sun? For companionship? Bees are genetically wired to search certain color patterns to find floral nectar. Have our minds been genetically wired to seek the heat of the sun, the warmth of a campfire comradery and the incandescent glow coming from the farmer's home? Are we genetically wired to love sunsets and sunrises?

Yes and no. Scientific apparatus such as EEG or PET will certainly show the glow of neural activity as we admire the sunset's color. Our brains are designed according to the human genome. But is there a mind beyond the measure of scanners? A strict empirical approach might suggest that by meditating on the rise or decline of sunlight we set our circadian rhythms and protect ourselves from overwork, insomnia and Seasonal Affective Disorder. But because mind and body are both the physical universe in the twilight zone the evidence is unclear. We find evidence for both a physical and a spiritual answer. We find evidence for God, and not for God; we find evidence of a soul, and not a soul.

> The path of the righteous is like the first gleam of dawn, shining ever brighter till the full light of day. But the way of the wicked is like deep darkness; they do not know what makes them stumble. —Pr. 4:18-19 NIV

It's harder for us to see the shades of beauty in sunrises and sunsets. In an essay entitled "Analog Art and Digital Art: A Brain-Hemisphere Critique of Modern Painting"[7] Paul Vitz, a psychologist at New York University, suggests that the best explanation for aesthetics must include a balance between the brain's need for analog and digital information, between right brain and left brain cognition. The left side is more rational and works to analyze the world into its simplest digital parts. The right brain makes analogies to what it sees. It finds tones and shades of meaning. The right brain enables us to make metaphors, similes, and to see the unseen and its meaning. Dr. Vitz believes that we are so much into the "Digital Age" that life has become meaningless. We are losing the ability to see mystery and profound beauty.

You can see digital thinking in our view of time. My great grandfather made a grandfather clock. Above the hands of time was a painted sky that rotated to place the course of the sun, moon and stars over the time of day. Each hour the chimes toll. Along the sides of the clock were Corinthian columns, symbols of reason and ancient wisdom. Its short legs were lions paws, another historical metaphor. The clock's time is analogue. My great grandfather lived in the time of ornate pocket watches and not digits flickering on a computer desktop. It was time changing from flickering candles to on and off incandescent lights.

We are now deep in the digital age. Time is a series of numbers crossing a screen. Time is more precise and more meaningless. There is less time for sunsets. Candles are for churches, not museums of modern art. The modern becomes as meaningless as some modern art, the lines and patches of paint define nothing.

Without faith, the pathos of good books, and sublime art displaying the colors and hues of sunrises and sunsets our minds drift toward the digital faiths of strict doctrines, mathematical precision and total predestination. Others drift to the right brain of irrationality embracing everything as it embraces nothing. Neither fulfills the whole brain faith of the Bible.

Strict fundamentalism and atheism prefers the strictly digital. Both prefer predestination more than the potential chaos of free will. Both believe that Genesis is written as science without shades of poetry. Both hold a zeal hostile to any opposition. Despite the indications of quantum mechanics they remain certain. God and the world are mechanically predestined like

Seeing the Unseen

the physics of an automobile crash. The light bulb is either on or it's off. They are either all wrong or all right. There is no glimmer of God's grace coming through the trees as English Landscape artist John Constable (1776 – 1837) painted it. Art is explanation and propaganda, not beauty.

We like a little darkness in our taste for books and movies. We can read or watch *Tales from the Dark Side* without fear that our neighbor is a flesh-eating abomination. We have faith that our neighbors are reasonable. Missionaries go even further. With confidence they even face martyrdom with hope. Yet on the other, far side, there are those who don't like the sunrise and sunsets. They prefer the darkness for its power to bring fear. Their names are recorded in history and literature: Iago, Jack the Ripper, Hitler, Richard III, Idi Amin, and Vlad the Impaler.

Others take time to meditating on those earthly hours of dawn.

I find this painting warm and peaceful. It's a light scape painted by Don Mayston (1923-2009), an RAF veteran of World War II. The landscape is of the River Deben, and the tide mill at

Woodbridge, a two hour drive from London. In the early morning our eye's color cells awaken. The bright colors of creation overcome the black and white of night (John 1:5). Farmers and fisherman start work under the visible signs of a new day. If it is warm, we go outside the office cubicle. Outside there's no light switch, only the natural rhythm of light and darkness. There's none of the dry carpet smell of ordered isolation.

We climb hills for Easter sunrise services. We await the dawn of a new day. Early Christian graves had an east-west orientation. The feet pointed east and the head west. At the resurrection the head rises from its peaceful rest (RIP) and faces East to greet Christ, "the sun of righteousness." Malachi 4:2 says, "But unto you that fear my name shall the Sun of righteousness arise with healing in his wings . . ."

We watch sunsets and get into the same reflective mood. The sun sets over New York Harbor. The painting is by American artist Sanford Robinson Gifford (1823-1880). His style is both of the Hudson River School of landscape painting and the Luminist. Like many landscapes there is a sense of time but also of travel. The sense of depth adds to the illusion of time and eternity. It is a fitting work to meditate on and remember. With depth and light it says that in this life we are here for a short time. Many nautical paintings of the nineteenth century and earlier are metaphysical. They ask ultimate questions. What is our final port of call? The grave? Or, another Kingdom? At twilight, light is disappearing. One can either look west and enjoy the rusty hues of sky above the setting sun, or turn 180 degrees and face the dark side.

Art and photography in offices, art galleries and in our homes enable us to pause and reflect upon what is the meaning and purpose of our lives. Their images remind us what matters. They beckon us to leave the television and the video games, go outside and see "what the Lord hath made."Ps 118:24 KJV.

Whether the beauty of sunrises, sunsets and all of creation is on our wall as art, on the mountain top, or by the sea, it can give us the joy and peace we desire. Besides restoring a degree of mental health, the aesthetics of creation remind us where our real future lies. Are we heading toward a new, resurrection day? Or are we facing a future of darkness, as Shakespeare defined as " . . . sans teeth, sans eyes, sans taste, sans every thing."

If your education and upbringing made you a cynic you may be thinking, "What's he talking about? It's just a sunrise and a sunset, light travelin' through the atmosphere. I don't see God in it."

We are surrounded by extraordinary beauty. All around the glory of God can be seen in nature's beauty. Some see. Some are blind. And some half blind.

Tree huggers and Pet-Loving Hermits.

In my art lectures I try to help people read paintings and photography. Artists try to show us how they see the world or how their patrons want us to see them. Christian landscape artists are more likely to paint man in harmony with nature. The human figures are ordinary people. Other artists please new age environmentalists paint and photograph a land devoid of people or populated by imaginary "noble savages." Their "Back to nature" is sometimes just "back off." They have faith that nature is tamer than the city. Some have been so foolish to think that love and patience will domesticate wild animals. Others just prefer a life with cats and dogs, lots of dogs, and lots of cats. I remember a former lawyer so ashamed of his alcoholism that he prefered the company of cats alone. Others ignore their children and grandchildren and prefer to raise dogs in their own image. Their dogs are eager to please. Unlike our children they can't make conscious reflection and think, "I'm not sure I agree with him. There's nothing wrong with barking at the mailman. But I have no desire to bite my fellow pit bull"

God's word of life confirms what we experience in life. The greatest beauty of God's creation arises from human hearts expressed in words and deeds. Parenting does include suffering love, but also greater joy. Immature love blossoms in the best of summer days. It knows none of the the joy in taking the worst of winter. Love always ends in pain. It may end in divorce or death. Many can't accept the terms of the kingdom of this world. Yet the Christian understands. Jesus loves us. Before introducing a great litany of suffering saints, The letter to the Hebrews (12:2) tells us that for the joy set before him Christ endured the cross. Christ reverses our pain and gives us life. The great divorce between Heaven and earth will end in the marriage of the lamb.

Living in the Twilight Zone

I can't understand the cynic's heart. They may be unwilling to see what they once saw as a child. It is just as likely that they've been coached that God is not like an eight hundred pound gorilla in the elevator. But do they really want a God who smacks us on the head with a twenty-pound Long Island bluefish to get our attention? Maybe they just need to look around. Maybe they just need a few more days to look and few days of creation to see it's the work of the grand Creator.

Yet it seems as though God has left us much in the dark. Why? Why is there just as much evil as there is good? The answer is in the story of Adam and Eve, and in the high drama of literature, even Shakespeare. Shakespeare intimidates many. Its language is a bit opaque and archaic, but its worth the study.

When director Steven Spielberg adapted the story of Oskar Schindler for film he chose the sharp outlines of black and white. There is a reason for this. Color often distracts from a universal message. Black and white film suits short stories and stage plays by creating an indistinct image. It's more like the mental images that we ponder in our hearts. Aristotle called mental images *phantasms*. The mind is the world of *fantasia*.

Mental images are intentional faded and not as clear as the physical world. If they were we would be utterly confused between reality and imagination. We wouldn't know if we were kissing Katherine Hepburn, Kim Novak or Elizabeth Quakenbush. As a former high school daydreamer, I wouldn't know if I was in Miss Malatesta's English class, fighting the Japanese in China, or walking along Egdon Heath in Thomas Hardy's *The Return of the Native*. For the sake of our sanity and our English grade our minds create a less colorful, less three dimensional world akin to black and white images. My generation remembers the dramatic black and white TV of television's "golden age." Even today I remember the messages in *Alfred Hitchcock Presents*, the *Philco Television Playhouse*, *Kraft Television Theater*, *Playhouse 90* and especially T*he Twilight Zone* . . .

Why did Rod Serling name his show *The Twilight Zone*? There are answers in the show's different introductions:

> You're traveling through another dimension — a dimension not only of sight and sound but of mind. A journey into a wondrous land whose boundaries are that of imagination. That's a signpost up ahead: your next stop: the Twilight Zone!
>
> You unlock this door with the key of imagination. Beyond it is another dimension: a dimension of sound, a dimension of sight, a dimension of mind. You're

Seeing the Unseen

moving into a land of both shadow and substance, of things and ideas. You've just crossed over into... the Twilight Zone.

Serling's words appeal to the psychology of Sigmund Freud, the science fact of Albert Einstein and the science fiction of Charles Howard Hinton (1853-1907). It is pure short story where things are not what they seem to be. Darkness appears as light. There's often a surprising twist at the end. The world is turned upside down. "It's twilight," the story says to us. Are these events, these characters directing us to light and life, or death and darkness? As the Good Book says, "be ye therefore wise as serpents, and harmless as doves."Matt. 10:16b KJV

One of the most popular of the Twilight Zone episodes, "To Serve Man" appeared on March 2, 1962. Nine foot tall aliens, called Kanamits, arrive on earth promising hope. Their heads are largely contoured around a super-brain and their faces

remain expressionless. They speak to us using voice synthesizers. They promise "to serve man" but we really don't know what's going on inside their hearts. What exactly do they have in mind?

Mr. Chambers, a decoding specialist for the U. S. military, searches for an answer by deciphering and interpreting an alien book. Aficionados of SciFi know better: "Don't trust those friendly critters." Christians know that the Devil himself can quote Scripture, "for Satan himself is transformed into an angel of light."2Co 11:14 KJV At first glance the fruit of the Kanamits looks good. The real question is what do they think of us? Friend or grits?

At the very beginning of the film Mr. Chambers tells us that a number people pondered in their hearts the alien visitors. They were not sure whether they were telling the truth, whether they were friend or enemy. In doing so earth projected a human quality in Kanamit intelligence: a heart. Hearts can be virtuous or devious (Psalm 101:2-4, Luke 8:15). If Kanamits can speak they can also lie. The words of their vocal synthesizers may not agree with the meditation of their hearts.

Animals don't conceal their feelings. Because man's heart is a function of a speaking mind, animals can't plot a false impression. They can't lie to you. You get what you see. But we have a neural heart chamber. We can plot our next move. We can decide to embrace the darkness or walk in the light. We can lie. And what about God? God has a heart also. Can He lie? No. "God is light, and in him is no darkness at all."(1Jn 1:6 KJV)

While God is light and has already separated the light from the darkness we live in a twilight universe, between two worlds. In the image of God we also have to separate the light from the darkness. It's our role in life to mature to full stature as children of God. We can either love the light or we can love the darkness. We can long for more light; we can hide from the light. The term "light" used in this paragraph and in most of Scripture is not waves of photons. It's about about the very "good" nature of God: His love, His righteousness. The light is the bright colors of God's character.

The Twilight of Science and Literature.

Just think for a moment about literature and drama. Aren't the works of the humanities all about living in the twilight zone, living in the shadow lands, somewhere between the pit and the city of God? In the twilight zone we exercise free choice. Creation is not self-interpreting. We need the Bible, God's nature guide. The world is a place, like the Garden of Eden, where God steps out and lets us make free moral choices. We are free to love him or turn our backs and face the darkness. He gives us a heart we can use to think before we act or speak. But that same heart can be deceptive. Many have a different private personae than the public one.

If you are interested in more physical light the best place to search for the light is the electric company, the hardware store, or a degree in physics. Some view consciousness, the mental heart, as entirely physical. The answers to life's problems are chemical and physical. Love, memories, joy, all thoughts and actions are purely mechanical and neuro-chemical.

Those who hold that consciousness is just physical live in inconsistency. How can they love someone? Do they kiss because it releases more neurotransmitters? What do they think of their religious neighbors? Is religion is a product of a diseased brain or a degenerate gene? If religion is genetic then do atheists have the degenerate gene? Is their focus on math and science causing atrophy of right brain functions? If logic is the cure for religion then, is atheistic logic the most logical? Considering the course of history and logic, isn't it better to say that the answer can't be resolved. We live in the twilight zone when it comes to the logic of religion and even science.

Drugs have great power over the mind for better or for worse. The same is true of literature. When we read a book and meditate on its meaning we grow brain cells. We alter our

Seeing the Unseen

thoughts and values. If we don't understand the book's meaning or purpose then it becomes another forgotten memory of our existence. If we read and approve of everything we read our life becomes aimless. Amoebic thinkers never mature.

You don't always need drugs to be healthy. You do need to avoid an unhealthy self-centered existence and read and listen for maturity. Ignorance is not bliss, neither is illiteracy. But living between light and darkness means "read with caution." Not all things are edifying.

In Milton's *Paradise Lost* again provides us a workable key:

> Fall'n Cherube, to be weak is miserable
> Doing or Suffering: but of this be sure,
> To do ought good never will be our task,
> But ever to do ill our sole delight,
> As being the contrary to his high will
> Whom we resist. If then his Providence
> Out of our evil seek to bring forth good,
> Our labour must be to pervert that end,
> And out of good still to find means of evil;

The ability to read, write books, compose new thoughts and speech from our lips is good. It is a gift from God. There are books full of light. Some start in the shadows and yet its final page turns us to the light. Not all books and ideas are good. Milton's poem has that caveat. In the shadow-lands where darkness and the angel of darkness remain there are books proclaiming truth that foster error, even evil. Discernment is called for.

We live in the shadows; our hearts are often double-minded. The best books have a touch of mystery about them. They use metaphors and similes to help us see. If you don't see the shadows and the light then you are not ready for the biographies of Robert Dallek and Doris Kearns Goodwin, nor the fiction of Shakespeare, Hawthorne, Melville, Flannery O'Connor, G. K. Chesteron and Phillip Roth. Yet even the spiritually blind still use the heart, God's gift enables us to read and discern Mickey Spillane, Ian Fleming and Dan Brown.

I have made bad purchases in the past. I was in a hurry. I didn't read the consumer reviews. I didn't ask myself, "Is this sale item really a bargain?" Or am I being deceived to buy a cheap knockoff? Sometimes a book on sale is only worth the paper it's written on.

On a trip to London I took a library book to read on the flight. The book's covers say that truth matters. Somewhere over the Atlantic I discovered that the author believes that there are no permanent, universal, or absolute truths. All is in a state of flux. The only long term truth is that there is no long term truth. It was an extra pound of useless baggage. I did have the sense to borrow and not buy the book.

Discernment, not book burning, is God's way. God gave us hearts to think about our decision, not matches. We don't burn books. Within the chambers of our heart we can meditate upon the words we read and hear. If your intent is honor, virtue and the love of God you will label some items as good, bad, and some a five out of a ten. Since evil's intent is to make evil out of good, the first steps away from God might come from a sermon devoted more to greed and vanity than glory. It may come from intellectual circles. Universities require that PhD theses be original. In theology and liberal arts that may mean garnishing data with sexist, racist, or fundamentalist conspiracy theories.

If you bought a bad book recycle the paper, don't recirculate it. Don't recycle library books. They are not your property. Start talking to people in the bus or plane in a gossipy manner about a "fabulous" book by Pasternak, Lewis, Walker Percy, King David or Dr. Luke.

Some Christian authors seem to have lost Jesus' message for the sake of popularity and riches. Many of them do good works but they present mixed messages. They preach love of presents more than love of the presenter?

I have a family from birth and from marriage. My heart often meditates about them. I was childish when I measured my parents' love by the gifts they gave me. I thought that Christmas and birthday gifts were the best blessings. Then I put away childish things. Now an Image of college days come to mind. My Dad visited me at school nearly every Sunday. He was sixty and semi-retired. We'd go to church and out to dinner at a nice restaurant. I could only afford the tip. After a while I calculated how much these dinners were costing him. I told him about my concern. We agreed to have dinner no more than every other weekend. But it was not the dinner he wanted to give; he wanted to give me himself. We made a compromise. Every other weekend he'd come early and have breakfast together. Coffee and fresh, hot donuts was a lot cheaper than dinner. It was the time together that mattered. The price of the meal was not the blessing. It was his presence. He's gone now. I wish I could go to his grave and shout, "Get up! It's Sunday, the Lord's day. It's time for coffee and donuts."

I ask my Heavenly Father for daily bread but more for His love, His wisdom, His presence. I am now the same age that my father was, those Sundays we had coffee and donuts. I thank God for the mind and muscles to work. I like working hard. I work hard whether I get paid too little or too much, whether my boss is Ebenezer Scrooge or old Fezziwig. At the end of the week I know that I had worked in a way pleasing to God. I get more pleasure out of God's presence than taking a nap in the stock room.

I look around me and see treasures that money can't buy. I have a great neighbor. I have a fellowship of Bible study friends that I treasure every Sunday. I enjoying being with my wife, even during 'differences of opinion.' I don't measure her by how much money she makes. I have rich memories and conversations with my children and all my kin.

When I asked God to help me share God's love in China, I imagined crosses above the heads of everyone, rich or poor, walking on Jiefang Road. God loves them much more than I loved my Dad. In China there are Christians who make modest amounts as physicians. There are others who live in poverty and suffering. They sing hymns with the same tone of enthusiasm and joy. Ironically the most joyous of American hymn singers are often those who just get by.

We know this. Jesus desired to do His Father's will even though He had no permanent place to lay his head. Yet I listen to a recording of a sermon given by a popular preacher. It's about dollar sign blessings. My heart asks, "Is this why we worship? Is this as *Paradise Lost* says, "out of good still finds means of evil"?

Mass media's insatiable need to fill their schedule with "wow" shows means junk, passing as truth. In Christmas 2009 there were a number of TV documentaries about Jesus' extended family. It was not as fictional as last year's *Davinci Code* hoax. Yet the programs promised secrets and confuse possibility with probability. Robert Beckford is a "Black theologian." His British Channel 4 Jesus' documentaries have titles using words like "secret," "hidden," and "decoded." The words hint at some grand conspiracies afoot. There is a catholic and orthodox reluctance to accept that Jesus had brothers and sisters. Only two of the four Gospels mentions Jesus' brothers and sisters. It hardly proves an embarrassing cover-up or a conspiracy. If that were the case all four Gospels would be devoid of these family references. Beckford goes on a fast chase to find names and facts about Joseph's family. The stories he collects are often too late to be taken as serious evidence. Yet Beckford says the stories are "probable." But when does the faintly probable become the possible?

Years after the Kennedy assassination people claimed to have seen a second gunman shooting at Kennedy from the "grassy knoll." As time went on, even the real witnessed spiced up their original accounts. There was fame and profit to be made. Writers made good money from these "eyewitness accounts".

But where do we get the real facts? Which books are we to read? Christians have guidance in the authority of Scripture as explained in 2 Timothy 3:16f. The verse says, "All Scripture is God-breathed and is useful for teaching, rebuking, correcting and training in righteousness so that the man of God may be thoroughly equipped for every good work."[NIV] There is also some guidance for reading in Philippians 4:8. "Finally, brothers, whatever is true, whatever is noble, whatever is right, whatever is pure, whatever is lovely, whatever is admirable—if anything is excellent or praiseworthy—think about such things."[NIV]

But what exactly does that mean? Does it mean that we can only read history and science books written by Christians? That hardly makes sense if you are a surgeon or an airline pilot. The textbooks and ongoing updated materials of these two professions are essential to good performance in medicine and aviation. As an auto driver I read the word "Stop." To act according to its message is "right." When it comes to reading literature and history we have a model in the literature of Scripture. David's Biblical biography is honest. It is not a political campaign biography. We read of a young boy who heroically takes on a bully more than twice his size. We also read of King David who stayed home when he should have been fighting for his country. He then goes on to adultery and murder. His repentant poetry is just as glorious as his praise tunes at the end of the Book of Psalms. The first chapter of Genesis, the temptations stories, and the Gospels are guidelines for finding good, honest fiction and history.

Honest history and literature are written in the gray areas of life lived in the twilight zone. I enjoy biographies of presidents written years after their presidency. Like the Gospels, biographies need a few decades to mature. Time filters between facts and fantasy, separates the irrational from the rational, and the essential from the trivial.

Biographies of John Fitzgerald Kennedy took time to mature. When Kennedy was assassinated I had just finished Victor Lasky's *JFK Man and Myth*. It was quite negative. The evidence was not manufactured. Lasky just left out the good parts. After Kennedy's death, biographers and publishers preferred the good parts only. The music of Lerner and Lowe's Broadway show *Camelot* became the theme of documentaries on the late president. Readers wanted to relive the Kennedy years as a happy Camelot kingdom. There's irony in this. The characters of King Arthur, Lancelot and Guinevere are from Sir Thomas Mallory's novel on the tragic consequences of adultery. By the 1980's the Kennedy biographies turned toward a more twilight image. The real JFK succumbed to the temptations of darkness and the honors of an enlightened nation.

False histories are not necessarily filled with lies, but with false impressions. They preach the bright side or the dark side of a nation's life. The dark sided histories are worse. They lead the reader to despair or its dark sister, the existential leap to nothingness. Their ultimate intention is chaos and the denial of hope and light. Their cynicism stops thinking and maturing.

Honest literature is filled with high drama. They help us to see the light in the dawn and the dusk of human life. True history searches for signs of faith, hope and love in the dawn and the twilight. We ought to honor Ken Burns and Geoffrey Ward more than Michael Moore. Faith and doubt pull consciousness toward the light of knowledge and wisdom.

I try to read reviews of history books before I buy or borrow them from the library. Unfortunately some history book begin with a strong political, preachy, bias. I have read portions of a well-known alternative American history. The book has some good elements. Yet the author admits gathering facts to prove his cynical convictions. It's not a good history to portray people as either good radicals or bad conservatives. There's no high drama in stereotypical characters. It stops students from further interest in history. It's like TV westerns where the bad guys wear black hats, the good guys where white hats.

I purchased and read *Flawed Giant: Lyndon Johnson and His Times 1961-1973* by Robert Dallek. Why? The title says it. There was light and darkness in the president. Dallek tries to " . . . explain how so self-centered a child, adolescent, and mature man was able to translate his neediness into constructive achievements that were the envy of healthier personalities. LBJ is an object lesson in the complexity of human behavior."[8] It is a great read. It's is a lesson book for all of us who are giants. Humility and honesty are essential.

Seeing the Unseen

Citizens need to have a common literature. Before the invention of printing press an entire community shared one or two pieces of literature. For the Greeks it was Homer. For the Jews it was the Bible. For Muslims it was the Qur'an. South Asians shared tales from Ramayana and Mahabharata. Egyptians read the Book of the Dead. They provided explanations to the cosmos and offered guidance. Sharing the same stories and traditional interpretations also created a unity and identity not shared in polyglot, multicultural societies. Making diversity primary means great information but less unity. The marriage of information and unity is possible and essential to the success of a nation. A healthy society reads widely and also affirms a few national or universal literary icons. But is there one book that can create unity and peace throughout the world? Is there a world book that isn't an Internet encyclopedia? And How is that book accepted as the world's? By the sword? By example? By persuasion? Or by love? The sword fails. Even a sword of Damascus steel or one made for the Samurai can't discern what a person really believes. Under the barrel of the gun Chinese people publicly praised "their glorious leaders" and cursed him in their hearts. The Quran, for example, must be accepted by example and in competition with other books. It does not say much for its merit that many Muslim countries make Bible reading and participation in alternative political parties a crime, even punishable by death. Let people decide for themselves which book is their religious text—which book(s) best describes their nations character.

Great thinkers and writers lived in a world of books. The students, that have the most original of essays and the highest grades without plagiarism generally live in a bookish home. Books, good reading, play a far more important part of their lives than TV. I have a picture of my bedroom taken in 1966. There are bookcases on the wall above my desk and a "The Solar System" poster is on the wall. On the desk is a clock radio, a radiometer, and a copy of Ebony Magazine. But next to the desk is a portable black and white TV. I didn't get to read all the books I wanted to. The books had to compete with Ed

Sullivan, Steve Allen, *Gomer Pyle USMC*, *Batman* and Walter Cronkite. I didn't go to Harvard or Yale. Instead I headed for the sunny skies of Marine Corps Depot, Parris Island. There I received a classic military education. It was not till I got out of the Marines that I underwent a renaissance of thought. I started to read more and ask, "Why?"

Arts Worth Meditating on

When I am jogging I hear music to keep an allegro or presto tempo. Audio books and classical music don't work. I can't seem to exercise my mind and jog at the same time. Without a conscious decision I shift down to walking. All the arts have items worth meditating up. Others are pretentious. Other items are shallow and merely appeal to emotions, sometimes to the most animal of our emotions.

Then there are the geniuses of the arts, too numerous to remember them all. I have my favorites. Yet much of today's art has become trivial. I am not sure we should call it art. A dictionary defines art as a skill. That means hard work and training. There's not much skill in today's pop, decorative arts. Art dealers tell me that decorative arts have replaced real art. The new art is really color schemes. Interior decorators and decorating magazines correctly teach that a bare beige wall needs a break of color. The decorators don't know your values, they want to sell arts that blend in, are nebulous, and commercially correct. They appeal to the vanity of approval: "Fabulous. Believe me. Your friends will love this." The unspoken word is mediocre, two dimensional flower paintings or Picassoesque harlequin copies. They are cheap and meaningless but better than a bare beige wall.

Children have a better idea about the purpose of wall art . . . meditation. Sons decorate bedrooms with images of sports cars, sports heroes, James Bond, high speed aircraft, or spicy girls. They do this because they want to meditate and "think on these things." (Philippians 4:8). Daughters may have more sentimental images and the youthful faces of pop super-stars. What in the family rooms are there to meditate? Earlier generations decorated their homes with family photos or portraits, landscapes of the old country, religious paintings, porcelain and book cases. They filled the parlor or family room with music coming from upright pianos and hi fidelity record players. It was always family music chosen by adult ears. Now in the privacy of their bedrooms, children and adults listen and watch from computers and personal TVs. The ignoble, dark angels of our nature make passionate, obsessive appeals. As any advertiser knows, you see and hear it enough times you buy it.

Vivaldi's *The Four Seasons* is not pop. It's serious. He created the music as a tone poem using various moods and sounds for each season. He meditated upon nature's sounds heard in the city of Venice. In the first printed score he tells us which images he has intonated with the notes and stops, with the timbre and voice of of various instruments. He pondered in his heart the mix of sounds and images to create a new thing.

The Heart and Others

In my youth there were many whose hearts were set on settling down with a partner, hopefully for life. It was about self-control, intellectual wit, good listening, being funny and polite. What happened in the 60's? Did our biologically brains suffer damage and lose sight of the non-biological? Or was it nurture? Or, was it both nurture and environment.

Civilization, child-rearing and marriage survive just as much by social bonds of civility as by fertility and good hunting. Drugs and good health care defeat infection and disease. Moral and intellectual civility defeat adolescent deaths from drugs, bullets and gas pedals. But where does this civility come from? It comes from words and a consciousness beyond the capacity of robotic and biological model. It is from the word. I do not mean a single word, but humanity, fashioned in the image of God, creating civil language. Civility is a nation's heart or mind separating the light from darkness, from good and bad language, life from death, light from darkness, just as God does.

I attended two high schools. I recall my best relationships with girls were much more about conversation than "hot stuff." I looked around at the happy couples, married for more than thirty years. It's about words not about turning back the clock with excessive make-up and plastic surgery. It's about speech pouring forth from the heart.

Purely biological neuroscience preaches a different gospel. When the senses stimulate the brain it creates a 'holographic representation' called consciousness. The brain does not make any intellectual, free will decisions, it merely follows the dictates of genetic variations in the human population and the accumulative affect of outside stimuli. The brain is genetically designed to look for a friendly face. What constitutes a friendly face is based on the volume of stimuli. A white face looks friendly in a white neighborhood; a black face is friendly in a black neighborhood. There's no heart, no free will. End of story.

Yet there is a problem with this purely biological approach. Our minds are not programed "to hate or to be "as wise and serpents and as harmless as doves." We have to be taught. Oscar Hammerstein II, a Lutheran and a Broadway lyricist, was right when he ironically wrote;

> You've got to be taught to be afraid
> Of people whose eyes are oddly made,
> And people whose skin is a diff'rent shade,
> You've got to be carefully taught.
>
> You've got to be taught before it's too late,
> Before you are six or seven or eight,
> To hate all the people your relatives hate,
> You've got to be carefully taught!

Is this biological? The song infers that we can be carefully taught to hate, or to love. Religion, literature and philosophy have done a better job of it than genetics and biology. It's not that science is immoral. It's just that biology is largely amoral. There's nothing in biology that tells us it's wrong to reduce green house gases by feeding belching cows and neighbors to the carnivores. Charles Dickens warned about the biological and the "survival of the fittest" model in his wondrous tale, "A Christmas Carol."

> "I wish to be left alone," said Scrooge. "Since you ask me what I wish, gentlemen, that is my answer. I don't make merry myself at Christmas, and I can't afford to make idle people merry. I help to support the establishments I have mentioned—they cost enough; and those who are badly off must go there."
>
> "Many can't go there; and many would rather die."
>
> "If they would rather die," said Scrooge, "they had better do it, and decrease the surplus population.

[Radio announcer: Ebenezer is in trouble, boys and girls. Who will save him from his nasty ways and make him a good neighbor? Richard Dawkins? Mr. Rogers? Or the Christmas child? Time is running out. Be sure to order the Dan Brown Secret Decoder Ring while supplies last. Tune in tomorrow for the further adventures of . . . *Charles Dickens in England!*]

Both the computer model and the biological model boil down to one assumption. The world, including the mind, can be explained by science. Science brings us certainly, mathematical certainties. The scientist becomes the new high priest of Gnosis. Only he can say for sure, "I know." There is a certain scientific arrogance that was once reserved for philosophers, Pharaohs, Kings and emperors, and unfortunately some leaders of Christendom. Scientists assumed their exalted position as early as the eighteenth century, and in most parts of the world by the twentieth. It promises calculable certainty. It is based on the mathematics of Newtonian physics, not on the atomic level of quantum physics that breeds uncertainty.

Some scientists preach that we don't have to get closer to God but we have to get closer to the god of the fixed, immutable laws of math and science preached by Spinoza, Einstein and Hawking. "God is love" has been been replaced by 'God is physics.' The high priests will give us light and save us all from ignorance. They even have the Holy Grail. It is not the legendary golden chalice that Christ drank from. Rather it is a lump of gray matter. In *Indiana Jones and the Temple of Doom*, the Thuggee priest holds a heart in his hand to prove that he has the power. It is a work of fiction from South Asian folklore. But today's practitioners of science gain a certain degree of respectability if they hold a brain in their gloved hands. Nathan Miller in his film the *Body in Question (1958)* opened up a cadaver skull to show the brain. Why? It's not rocket science to know that the brain is inside our thick skulls.

In a BBC film production *The Secret You.* mathematician Marcus Du Sautoy attempted to find evidence that the 'I' can be explained mathematically and scientifically. He asks a brain scientist if he can hold a human brain. Was it for high drama or to assert his credentials? The outward visible sign of the inner discoveries of neuroscience is the priest holding a human brain. He's got the whole cognitive world in his hands. Du Sautoy has earned cognitive legitimacy. But has Du Sautoy's quest for the brain's 'I' given us any more truth than we had before? His brain is scanned. The images are sharper and clearer than x-rays. Resonate imaging has replaced EEG scripting. It provides a more precise location for mental activity. We are told that science is getting closer to the truth of the mind. But mid-twentieth century science already knew that thoughts come in stereo. Since the 1920's researches knew that thoughts emanate from different parts of the brain. Have we really learned that much more about consciousness and the heart?

In the Western religious tradition, priests and rabbis can exercise their thoughts with smugness, or with humility. Religious humility honors good science and good government without idolatrous prostration. And what of the new priesthood of science? Some of their academic acolytes mock any notion that is not scientific, They pretend to be be blind to the historic benefits of religion and philosophy. Their promised scientific breakthrough discovery of memory and the real "I," has proved to be an empty chalice. We can hold the brain in our hands, but the mind still eludes us. Has God kept the answer from the five senses?

We live in days of evening and morning, where the most enlightened of sacred and secular scholars are still in the dark. The clear enlightenment of noon-day sun as hoped by scientists since the eighteenth century is as impossible as the nonfiction colonization of another star system. The mass/energy physics of the universe does not allow it. Neither does the mind, what the Bible calls the heart, give up its secrets. The answer, like death itself, is now a wall of silence. For the sacred believer there is an ancient prophecy: "They will not need the light of a lamp or the light of the sun, for the Lord God will give them light. And they will reign for ever and ever."—Rev. 22:5

The Heart is a Home.

When I was in college I read a booklet entitled "My Heart Christ's Home" by Robert Unger.[9] For decades the response Gospel message has been to "ask Jesus in your heart." Unger's analogy of the heart as a home is befitting with the real intent of the heart. It's not just inviting Jesus into our hearts but the entire Christian life as well.

> That he would grant you, according to the riches of his glory, to be strengthened with might by his Spirit in the inner man; That Christ may dwell in your hearts by faith; that ye, being rooted and grounded in love, [Eph 3:16f NIV]

The word "dwell" means that God means to live there in our hearts, what the earlier verse calls the inner man. How can it be an "inner man" and a dwelling place for Christ?

Seeing the Unseen

To helps us to understand how the heart can also be called the inner man I turned to that great Catholic scholar . . . Alfred Hitchcock. You may have rented or purchased Alfred Hitchcock's film *Vertigo* (1958) because you heard that it was an exciting drama. But a closer examination reveals a message about life, about passion and the dangers of misdirected meditation. An image, a fantasy, and obsession kills. Guarding our hearts and filling it with honor and virtue brings life. The film is a visual sermon about art and meditation.

Detective John Ferguson, played by Jimmy Stewart, is investigating Madeleine Elster, played by Kim Novak. Madeleine's husband Gavin tells Ferguson that she's suicidal and possessed with the thoughts of Carlotta Valdez, a dead woman. Carlotta killed herself nearly a hundred years earlier. It's Detective Ferguson's job to watch her. In one scene Ferguson follows Madeleine to the California Palace of the Legion of Honor, an art museum. Madeleine sits before a painting of Carlotta and meditates on her image.

It is an illusion in a number of ways. An actress is acting like another woman looking carefully at a painting. Later we learn that the fictional character Madeleine is not really meditating on the painting in the way that Gavin Elster suggests. She is not possessed by its image. She is not even Gavin Elster's wife.

Seeing the Unseen

She is pretending. We don't know what actress Kim Novak is thinking. She may be thinking about lunch or the next day's shooting. But Ms. Novak is a woman acting like a woman acting like she's meditating on a painting.

Director Alfred Hitchcock widens the frame. Now Madeleine is in the background and Inspector Ferguson is in the foreground. Here is illusion again. We watch Jimmy Stewart watching Kim Novak watching a painting. Later, in our mind we can watch a phantasm image of Jimmy Stewart watching Kim Novak watching a painting and wonder what's the story about.

Through the camera lens and through Stewart's extraordinary performance we know more about Detective Ferguson's heart. At first Ferguson, or "Scottie," is just doing his job as a detective. He's trying to uncover the truth about her sanity, meditating on every step she takes. We also know that he has other thoughts. Scottie is single. He's not interested in his friend Midge, a modern sensible girl whose idea of sexuality is without mystery. From the day he first saw her profile at Earnie's Restaurant his heart was set upon her as a lovely woman and the mystery he craves. His meditations become an obsession. His mind crosses over the line between reality and fantasy, between reasoning and obsessing. In the end both John Ferguson and Madeleine tragically suffer. They both suffer because the words of her mouth and the meditations of her heart are different.

In film, the art gallery is a metaphor for the heart meditating on visual images and memories. We have the historical memory of Carlotta Valdez and her painted image. Madeline's heart appears to be focused upon a moment in the past, a dead past. We have Scottie looking into the gallery meditating on her gaze and trying to discern her thoughts.

Through the eye of the camera lens Hitchcock directs our meditations on what we just saw and to make sense out of the story. He wants us to meditate for 122 minutes in the theater and be haunted by the film.

"What's in your wallet?" one company advertises. A far more important question is, "What's on your mind?" What do you treasure there? What art, memories of the past, written words do you keep on permanent display in the gallery rooms of your heart? In Matthew 6:21 Jesus says, "For where your treasure is, there your heart will be also. " Jesus says that the eyes are as a lamp to the body. It is a metaphor. So also is the light or darkness that eyes take into the body. On a purely physical level our eyes don't take in darkness. We sometimes talk about good light and bad lighting. But good eyes take to heart all that is good. Whatever the eyes see or ears hear first enters the brain before the rest of the body acts. Whenever we read books or hear stories about what good is, the more we readily act in a good way. When we prefer the darkness of vanity, racism, hate, greed, and the love of money, we darken our lives. We stop seeing the goodness of God's creation. We see the absence of good and God.

When Christ dwells in our hearts there's a another voice interrupting and interfering with our bad ideas. We can listen and honor his presence or ignore Him. We can let Jesus and the Spirit of God be upon the memory galleries of our heart.

Seeing the Unseen

The Mind as a Memory Gallery.

Another Catholic writer, with more sacred credits to his name, saw consciousness as a memory gallery. He is well known even in Communist China. His name in Chinese is Li Madou. His Italian name is Matteo Ricci (1552-1610). Ricci astounded the Chinese court by mastering written, classical Chinese in a matter of a half dozen years. He did this by creating in his heart mnemonic palaces. Each room became a visual exhibition for Chinese vocabulary. To refresh his memory on a particular word or phrase he merely had to enter one of his mental chambers. He didn't try to lean the language by staring at a bilingual dictionary. Instead he acknowledged that the brain's memory is primarily an inner, three-dimensional chamber. We can meditate by entering each memorable room over and over again. In today's parlance, the heart serves as an enormous film library containing popular referenced films/memories and rarely opened film canisters that seem like uncatalogued clutter.

The Haunting Meditations of War

I love paintings and good photography. Near my writing desk is book of the panographic photography of Ken Duncan. Whether it be a Kansas field of sunflowers or the fall leaves in the Vermont countryside, the photos provoke thoughts in accord with God's. We see the natural beauty and also declare it good. Nearly fifty years ago I had come across a copy of Edward Steichen's photo book *The Family of Man* (1955). One photo in the book, by Al Chang, is of a soldier receiving comfort from another during the

Korean War. His best friend has died. I have often looked at the photo and thought about the two men. They know that death is maddening. In the face of death an embrace of life is the best comfort.

In combat the man in your fire team, your friend, may die inches away. You could be next. Some men cope by not thinking about it. They have that thousand-mile stare. Others meditate on life. Sure their friend is gone, blown to bits, but you remember and meditate on him alive. The trenches of the First Great War (1914-1918) produced many marked by the worst signs of what was first labeled as shell shock. The term was misleading. There were places and occasions where shelling was severe. But just as severe to the psyche was staying in the trenches next to the decaying remains of a former comrade. Killing the enemy face to face challenged the inner conscious of those raised in a landscape of Christian virtue. For these men there were no antidepressant drugs. The cure was words, getting men to talk out their feelings and having them meditate on life. The cure of the heart is a turn to light and life of this world and the next.

But what are the faithful to talk about? We, enlightened by the Word and the Holy Spirit, talk "good" talk." God's intent is that the self talk, the meditations of the heart, separates the light from the dark side that exists in this world and turns to the the light and the coming Kingdom of God.

I like to talk about photography and art. When I was eleven years old my father took me to the Museum of Fine Arts in Boston. I remembering being surprised by a near life size painting by William Singer Sargent, *The Daughters of Edward Darley Boit* (1882).

Seeing the Unseen

Three of the four girls seemed to be staring at me. All four looked alive. It was an illusion just as the painter had created the illusion of three dimensions on a two dimensional canvas. At eleven I knew that people had lived and died before I was born. But now I knew what that means. They think and stare at faces like I do.

That painting got me hooked on art. I enjoy looking through art books and reading about the history of the paintings. I have visited many of he great art museums in the United States, China and England.

I am now quite particular about what paintings I spend my time with. Here are two entirely different paintings, neither one have I actually seen . . .

Seeing the Unseen

The one on the left is Jackson Pollock's *Fathom Five.* (1948). I look at it and think, "Ah, what's this about and why did someone pay big money for this (a reported 140 million dollars in 2006)?"[10] It was apparently bought as an investment and not something the owner intends to admire. I don't think much about its meaning. It has no meaning. The other is Rembrandt's *The Return of Prodigal Son* (1662). Rembrandt struggled in his heart between faith and vanity. While painting this work he was old, nearing death. His heart had made a decision. Meditating on earlier messages and memories he began to seek eternal glory. The work is in St. Petersburg, Russia and in my heart nearly every day. Nearly every day I ask myself which one in the painting am I? Am I repentant of my sins to God? Am I doing the will of my Father who is in Heaven? Or am I like the other son? I have seen that's son's face before. It is that same indifferent look of those who watched Jews suffering in the camps and on the streets of Warsaw and Berlin. As a Christian I ask myself, "Which one of them am I today?

Because we are created in the image of God, we are fashioned to make moral and aesthetic decisions. Animals have some sense of the aesthetics but its more a case of tranquility, freedom from hunger or fear. We have that and much more. We arrange our gardens and we decorate our homes. We search for the best books to read, the best films to see, the best music to hear. When it is a healthy search it creates emotional stability and maturity.

As creative speakers and writers we have words. Words, words, and more words! We are created in image of God's eloquence and creativity. Jews and Christians, having been enlightened by the written word of God, should be the most creative speakers and writers. Over the course of two millennia this might well be true. Think of the names of these great writers: S. Y. Abramovitsh (a.k.a., Sholem Eleichem), Tolstoy, Dostoyevsky, Asa Gray, Samuel Taylor Coleridge, Isaac Babel, Michael Faraday, Solzhenitsyn, Phillip Roth, Chesterton, C. S. Lewis, Elie Wiesel, Charles Dickens, Spencer, and William Shakespeare. They believe or accept a Biblical world view.

And what about this present generation? We, who have been raised to life in Christ, raised in Christian homes, raised in the poetry of Christian worship, should be the most bookish of souls, the most learned of scientists. We should be lovers of words, word smiths forging and sculpting metaphors, parables and inspiring others to lift hearts and voices to God.

Well it hasn't happened, at least not in America. Why? Over the past fifty years in American life you can find the reasons why. We have no time to write and read much. We are spellbound to advertising images, fast-acting flicks and flat screened TVs. We don't read Shakespeare we copy a "Wiki" synopsis of the bard's legacy. Religious spokesmen speak soundbites promising enough blessings to buy big, BIG houses, big cars and an even bigger home entertainment centers. In our living rooms, friends and family compete for speaking space with TV superstars, even a cute green lizard selling insurance.

Many American and English Christians have abandoned positions as leaders and standard bearers of word greatness.

We are afraid of being labeled elitists. We don't sit and read our Bibles. We quip a few verses. Some of us draw attention to our cause by inscribing cross tattoos, hip-hop talk or self-help promises to the worshipers of easy success. We call both styles as 'relevant' and yet it bears a message of sameness. It's all outward.

Forget the clothes and the hip-hop jive. Talk real. At a ball game I sat next to a young man who loved his beer, and proclaimed his identity with a light green Mohawk hair style. If I wanted him to know God's love my hair cut makes little difference. I smiled and asked if he thought my wife would like me better if I got a Mohawk too. He roared with laughter. He suggested the reverse. We shared names and baseball talk. When the game was over, I just said what was true and in my heart, "It was great talking to you, God bless you." And, he said the same in return. I didn't give him the "divine insurance salesman" hustle. I treated him for who he was, a man created in the image of God. Sure I prayed. I prayed that somewhere in Georgia another part of God's church would help him take the next step to seeing who he really is: a divine image, an image who may have stepped out of the God's light, a man whose ultimate destiny is not to fall "dust to dust" but to be raptured and conformed in the image and likeness of God's only begotten Son. All the steps are undertaken are prescribed in The Holy Bible with a richness of insight, a treasury of words and an abundance of life.

When God spoke He changed the course of matter into a habitation, and then nature into life. He saw that it was "good." What did God mean by good? Here 'good' is an adjective. It is not a thing, it is a quality. God describes the work of every creation day as 'good' except one, the second day. Why is that day excluded from the category of good? The seas and the air created have one thing in common to human existence: You can't live there without taking part of the dry land with you. The pilot and the passengers of an airliner sit 'inside' an earthly tent of metal. The same is true of submariners and seafarers. Without some form of earthy habitation we either fall from the sky or drown. With the exception of those two locations, all of creation the earth and all animals are 'good' for human life. Yet in the creation we have to use words like 'good' and 'bad.' We have to separate the light from the darkness and call the light good and the darkness . . . nothing good. We have to appropriate such words as good and evil, tame and dangerous, light and darkness from our hearts and minds because the Scripture tells us that creation is not in all the good and the light of God's Kingdom. This earthly life is within the high drama of "The Twilight Zone."

Separating the Light from the Darkness

Any word must have its opposite in order to have meaning at all. Living is defined by activity but also by death, its absence. One must also define good by its absence: bad or evil.

As a young father I used to create simple sand sculptures for my two daughters and our foster children. Whether I created a crocodile or a sand castle I inevitably created a pit, the abyss. When the stars, planets and other celestial objects were formed, part of the universe became darkened and more vacuous. Every object in the universe is defined by what it is and what it isn't. While darkness is the absence of light, without darkness, light would be meaningless.

Light and darkness are typological images of the absence and presence of God. The Biblical idea of light is typologically associated with good and with life. We sing, "This little light of mine; I'm goin' to let it shine" and even the child understands we are not talking about candlepower, not so many lumens of light energy. We are talking about a moral, Godly goodness that we should not hide under a bushel basket.

The ending of the Bible, is also the end of God's symphony. It's not a tragic end of stellar fusion energy. In Revelation of St. John the end will be heavenly: "There will be no more night. They will not need the light of a lamp or the light of the sun, for the Lord God will give them light. And they will reign for ever and ever. " Rev 22.5 NIV

Revelation says "the Lord will give them light." Compared to their pagan contemporaries the Jewish prophets did not confuse God with light. They did not confuse creation with the creator either. Pagans worshiped the sun as god and some even regarded darkness as a spirit presence. But the Jews saw themselves in a realm of spiritual obscurity. Here in this world is both darkness and and light. It is twilight. Some love the light and some prefer the darkness. Psalm 82:5 says of the wicked, "They do not understand; they wander in darkness.". While the world God created pours forth speech it is obscured by the darkness.

But there is hope. Paul tells us that even the the unrighteous can at least see God's invisible attributes, His eternal power and divine nature. They see it from what God made. Then Paul goes on to say that Pagan thinking became nonsense when it worships creation.

The Scripture does not take a lot of time to explain the why of some things. The cause of blindness is perhaps given in the account of man's exile from Paradise. Even by the reckoning of Jews in the time of Moses, Paradise, the Garden of Eden, was not the whole world. It is the land between the Tigris and the Euphrates. It is a place of blessing. There are trees pleasing in appearance and good for food (Genesis 2:9). There was work there but it was work that pleases us (2:15). Then man made a fatal choice. They were expelled from Paradise. We now live in a hostile world that yields fruit in the midst of thorns and after painful labor. In Milton's *Paradise Lost*, the fall brings thorns to the rose. But if it is Paradise, why is God not there when the serpent temps the first couple? Why is the serpent there at all. Aren't snakes predators?

From much of Christendom's history the answer is self-evident to true lovers. You can't have true love without free will. If there is a shotgun at the wedding it's not about love. In the Jewish Hassidic interpretation free will comes because God separated the light from the darkness. Where God dwells there is no darkness. It's the pit left after the sand castle is made out of the dust of the earth. It's dark and foreboding in a child's eyes. We hear voices in our hearts from both ends of the moral yardstick. Now is the hour of decision which way do you choose?

Conclusion . . . Love at First Sight

> i thank You God for most this amazing
> day:for the leaping greenly spirits of trees
> and a blue true dream of sky;and for everything
> which is natural which is infinite which is yes—E. E. Cummings

Some time in the midday of my youth I laid down on uncut grass and sedge. I was an "explorer" who'd journeyed beyond home to a vacant lot just down the street. I set my right eye down low enough to see blades of grass like stalks of sugar cane. Late Summer grasshoppers snapped hind legs and attempted to vault over me, the humongous hominid. A foraging party of ants scurried along dirt paths bearing bits of twig and leaf. It was "High Def" nature without the BBC voice of Richard Attenborough. It was a microbial odyssey . . . better than watching the world pass by in Dad's '54' Chrysler, behind a wall of auto safety glass.

Then I turn on to my back, closed my eyes and listened. Nothing. I felt the tickling blades underneath. Sunlight opaquely passed through closed, sleepy lids. It seemed like the joy of death at the dawn of heaven. I still enjoy resting in fields undisturbed, neither by power mowers, nor by cow and canine pies. Fifty years later, eyes opened or shut, I can recall that vacant lot as yesterday. It is a treasured memory.

Both silence and sound have their ecstasies. Over time I have collected and treasured the sound of a rake scratching against the sidewalk, the stinging, whispers of New England

Seeing the Unseen

winds dusting snow on hands and face, the faint whirring sound of maple seeds rotating and descending and strumming along streets and sidewalks, sacred hymns, operatic arias, instrumental pieces. There are songs and singers I listen with a deep breath to hold back tears. There are vibrations just like the strings of a violin. Their melodies resonate chords of the heart, stirring recollections of home, courage, faith, hope and love.

In a regrettable moment I forgot these memories. By then I was in high school. I knew the parts of a grasshopper. I had already dissected a worm and a spiny sea urchin. I was losing sight of the whole picture.

My mother came back from hospital. She was dying from cancer. I remember it was a warm fall day when she asked me to sit with her in our small back yard. She looked up at the trees, down at the grass and said, "Oh, isn't it beautiful."

"What's beautiful?" I thought. The backyard consisted of uncut, weeds, grass and sedge. We didn't have a lawnmower; we spent our money on food . . . not on grass seed or turf builder.

Years later I realized my mistake. For an immature, adolescent time I had lost sight of what I once saw. My mother saw 'me' and the grass of the fields for what it is: "the finger play of God." I had lost sight of the joys of creation.

Seeing the Unseen

Here are the works of two artists. One is by 16th century European artist, Albrecht Durer (*Large Turf*, 1503). The other is by 20th century Chinese artist Ms. Jiang Caiping (*Remembering Banna*, 1995). Both are representation art. Both required the artist's intense meditation. Both show the essence of what my mother saw, what I could not see in 1965. I saw in part as a child and now see better each passing day of my old age.

On a scientific, evolutionary level we might not see what we ought to see. The sight of beauty and awe are unnecessary in the "evolutionary" survival of the species. Animals have no need to experience awe and joy. Is it only in anthropomorphic family films that dogs and cats climb hills to admire the view. Do we need such sentimentality? YES!

Why do our brains hold on to these images so near to the surface of the cerebral cortex, so near to our recollection. Why? Why in moments of presumed immanent death do survivors see some memories past pass before them? Are happy moments stored in cerebral folds to be resurrected at the hour of our death so that we might "go gently through the dark night?" Are joyous memories analgesics against mortal fear and panic? In the SciFi film *Soylent Green* (1973) natural beauty is a thing of the past. The character played by Edward G. Robinson spends his last moments in a euthanasia clinic. He is comforted by images of nature displayed on a flat screen TV.

In real life Robinson, one of Hollywood's masterpiece performers, was in the last stages of terminal cancer. He was not entirely acting. If you look at the film, look also at his facial expressions. He seems far more thankful than comforted. Like the Genesis creation story, Robinson's character finds nature's beauty as a sign of the goodness of creation . . . something worth an eternal memory. His life fades into a video sunset.

Flowers in a hospital bedroom just as much as the smiling presence of friends prove cathartic. They don't help the dying to turn and face a darkened door of death. They declare hope and eternal life. The funeral home does a good job making the body look alive. It reminds us of life, not of corruptible death.

Seeing the Unseen

Only among the most irrational and corrupt is death devoid of flowers and joyous eulogies.

As I grow older I find the aggregate of joy far more personal. Memories of friends and persons that mattered in my life come in moments of tranquil reflection. These memories draw closer and parallels the present. They have become more like the love songs or advertising jingles that played over and over in my adolescent head. Now I hear and see Joe, my next door neighbor in graduate school opening the door of his home and calling for his dog, "Lady!" That was thirty years ago. I see my daughter talking about the gentle monsters who live behind the bushes. That was twenty five years ago. Years earlier I see my sister Shirley and my Dad greeting me after graduating from Marine Corps boot camp.

I hear and see Cliff Collins telling me how he gained faith in God as a combat soldier on a Korean hillside. He died suddenly, about fifty years of age, too young to see his grandchildren. I have a photo of him in front of the Episcopal Church we attended together. It is just a side view of him talking to someone outside the camera frame. As I look at this fading colored photograph I wish he'd turn around and let me tell him how much I loved him as my elder brother.

I was the last person to see Beulah Baker alive. She was born near the beginning of the twentieth century. In the late 1970's she played the piano in a small church, less than a hundred attending. Her taste in music was more for the traditional, gospel hymns. She admitted it. Yet she told us that she thanked God that our guitar-sung, photocopied, praise hymns drew young people closer to the Lord. She was just an older, more mature believer than the rest of us. She had developed breathing problems from years working in a bank scented with second-hand smoke. But she still seemed to gleam with a childlike, joyous grin. On the last day of her life I drove her home to her senior citizen apartment. Just before she got out of the car she turned to me, smiled, winked and said, "You know I'm not afraid to die."

Seeing the Unseen

As I drove home I kept thinking how odd for her to say that. Two days later Tom Perkins, a leader in the church, informed me that Beulah had died in her sleep that same Sunday night I had taken her home. God had gone further. He had taken her to her eternal home. At the funeral Pastor Jeff Marx admitted that she had been more the spirit of the church than him. This was no false humility. Jeff had taught us; Beulah had shown us. She is another collected memory. Friends, sisters, my parents, my wife and children, even strangers bring the greatest joy. The memory does not so much comfort or allay a fear of death. They salt my heart to thirst again for those personal encounters.

My children live in a different U. S. state than I. Yet I see them everyday. At night and as the alarm awakens I see their faces in different scenes and in different ages. My parents and three sisters make their appearances on the mental stage nearly every day.

Why is it that we fail to give thanks to them or to God for the gifts of lives we encounter? At their funerals we weep, or meditate on the life insurance policy, wishing we had one or the other. We really need the mortician make them alive, just one more time, just one more memory to hold.

Are we just too busy, having too many things? Are there just too many people walking in and out, taking up much of our time, not lingering long enough to make bonds of friendship and love?

Without public TV and the Discovery Channel how many of us would see nature's wonder . . . what earlier generations saw every day? The scenery quickly passes by. We drive to another destination. We meditate on having too much money, or too little. Family, friendship, love and beauty, our core values pass us by. We're too busy to read a good book. We rush around hoping to have a few slow, cherished moments. We don't see the simple things, a small bookshelf of best books, a photo album of family and friends, paintings, our back yard. Even a few favorite films can help us pause, remember, reflect and sculpt our souls into what we ought to be and what we chose as our future.

Seeing the Unseen

There are moments, what Rudolf Otto called the 'numinous' where we see the unseen, something we might call breathless beauty, awe, the majestic, the holy. It's something seen by all cultures. It's often misunderstood, or misdirected to the worship of flimflam charlatans and kings. It is something our senses sometimes see and our minds barely comprehend. It is acknowledged in the Upanishads, pondered by ancient Greeks, extolled by Sufi poets, and mystic writers such as Meister Eckhart:

> Upon this matter a heathen sage hath a fine saying in speech with another sage: "I become aware of something in me which flashes upon my reason. I perceive of it that it is something, but what it it is I cannot conceive. Only me seems that, could I conceive it, I should comprehend all truth.[11]

The "flashes" are there, but humanity's interpretations are muddled in philosophies and religions. We expect a simple key, simple guiding words of explanation that all of us can understand. Instead the world give us condescending "enlightened" gurus, reincarnations and "anointed" super spirits. They expect worship, critical acclaim and money. Their teachings are sometimes fatuous and often wrought with contradictions. To preserve their place in the hall of idolatry they speak words intentionally incomprehensible to children and adults alike. The prefer long titles and just as long robes, like the emperor's new clothes.

There's a far simpler answer to our sense of awe and joy. It's a line from a poem, from a good book . . . The Good Book . . .

> *And God saw every thing that he had made, and, behold, it was very good.*
> — *Genesis 1:31*

Chapter Nine

Creating an Educational Environment

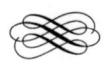

When we gives thanks for our daily bread we unconsciously take this is a metaphor for everything. I'm not sure that is the case. The Scriptures provides us with images of drought and famine in Biblical places. In such places and in such times, you thank God that there is bread. The bread is life. Breaking the loaf and sharing it will the family is a very happy thing. The family knows that they will not starve today. But we in the west unconsciously accept the relative wealth of the Middle Class as the minimum standard. Anything less we blame God.

Much of our daily life is ruled by unconscious impressions from our environment. Mom and dad read books, there are books and bookshelves everywhere. They love, forgive and enjoy talking. Their children will grow up to enjoy learning, have a happy marriage. It's not hereditary, it's an environment.

Another mom and dad fight all the time. They sit around and watch TV. Their marriage ends. Their children will grow up bored with education, expecting a happy marriage but unconsciously accepting arguments and divorce as the way to go. The cure for these children is noble meditations arising from the heart.

Twenty minutes in a home and you can tell whether younger members in the family will go on to college and graduate school.

Seeing the Unseen

The clues are in the sights and sounds and space. Is the living room just a TV room? A multimedia entertainment center? Are there bookcases, reading lamps and comfortable chairs for people to read? Does the room say, "Read, think, enjoy." Are there any bookcases and books that awaken the heart to think? Since I have already defined 'heart" as thinking, books and all literature should preach two words to the eyes "Read me!" Children's books, books on airplanes and automobiles, a dictionary, short stories collections, poetry, favorite novels and photo albums draw the eyes of family and friends to read. The complete collection of Harold Robbins novels or a multi-volume collection on the art of macrame are too sexist or too specialized.

In homes where men and women live in harmony expect biographies, art and history merged to form a bound panorama of faith and Americana. Keep specialized books away, in a special room. A good family bookshelf says to family and friends welcome. Stacks of books on theoretical physics or urology in the living room are intimidating. They don't say "welcome."

I remember seeing a home where living room shelves were filled with bound copies of *Playboy*. In another computer/electronic books and magazines filled living room and dining table. The room's message: "Dad's trade school job rules."

Classrooms are homes to educate our children what is important. When I grew up pictures of the George Washington, Abraham Lincoln where clearly displayed in nearly every classroom. Years later I saw one history classroom devoid of presidents and heroic leaders of the past. Instead there was a large poster of the Barry, Robin and Maurice Gibb, *The Beg-Gees*.

Paintings or photographs on the walls should entertain the memory and imaginations for all. There's nothing wrong with decorative art, flat unskilled images of flowers, old buildings or big-eyed babies and dogs. But they are not memorable. Photos help us to find the real beauty that God created for us to enjoy. I enjoy seeing a wall covered with family portraits. Even more wondrous is a photo of the family decades earlier "in the old country."

Seeing the Unseen

    A coffee table is all educational if it has coffee table books. Place there Photo albums, and photo books with lots of pictures. They start great conversations and get people into reading. Which paintings? That depends on how far along you are in seeing the beauty. We usually think of beauty in waterfalls, fields of flowers, dolphins and whales leaping between sky and sea. Yet the grandest joy, the greatest beauty, and the greatest loves comes from people. Granted people can deceive, they can bite and can kill like a grizzly. But the greatest rewards of beauty come from people just like us.

    If you want your child to be a Olympic swimmer take them to a lake or a swimming pool. You want them to become a great fisherman? Take them to where's the fish are biting. If you want them to learn in school take them to a used bookstore. You want them to serve and love God take them to nursing homes, where people are in need and in churches where love acceptance and forgiveness are clearly visible. You want them to have happy marriages? Give them a place to see.

Appendix 1

Educating Images and Ideas for Meditation

～⧖～

Anthony has had a double bypass. He's forty-five pounds overweight and he takes pills for high blood pressure. Anthony and I are about the same age. I exercise and enjoy running down to the local gas station for a cup of coffee. I wrestle with a few pounds around the middle but my heart is strong, sturdy and and ready for an aerobic rock. I am in much better shape than Anthony. But in terms of eternity Anthony's heart may be better than mine. In God's eyes, tight abs and aerobic exercises of the heart are not as important as exercising the heart in my head.

> Why should you be beaten anymore? Why do you persist in rebellion?
>
> Your whole *head* is injured,
> your whole *heart* afflicted. —Isaiah 1:5

In the verse the prophet Isaiah places the very heart of man in his head. When Jesus spoke the parable of the sower and the seed in Matthew 13, he doesn't initially explain it. He wants the disciples to think by meditating his earthy images in their hearts. Jesus explains that the various soils are various ways to take to heart the word of God. There were probably listeners to Jesus' parable who walked away indifferent to its hidden meaning. They are the hard soil. The disciples have at least past the first part of a mental test. They want to know what's the meaning. But once understood the meaning has to have room to grow in the heart.

Later Jesus tells us that the various soils represent various attitudes toward God's word. Hard soil does not accept the seed. It produces nothing. This is the mind of the cynic, but not always that of the skeptic. A cynic, however, will back away from God's power when God shows His hand with plagues. In the story of Exodus, Pharaoh's was already a cynic when Moses first spoke to him. Yet his hard heart was strengthened in order that God's glory might be revealed.

The mind processes what you see, hear, smell and touch. It's your mind where you treasure and meditate upon the past and the present. Our thoughts and thinking are the very heart of who we are. What matters more is what you put in your mind than what you put in your stomach.

When you lose your job, does your mind think of the loss or the future?

When a relative dies do you think about the will, the 1972 Gran Torino in his garage, or the life lost?

Whether you end your life in the brotherhood of the grumpy or in the presence of the angels depends on what your mind goes over and over again. Having read a bit about memory I've made up a "Rule of Nines." Your mind can't remember more than nine memories in any category, at any one time.

The clearest example of this phenomena is our sense of our own history. You may have heard or said something like this: "It's seems like Yesterday I graduated from Franklin D. Roosevelt High. That was forty years ago." We sense that time quickly passes by because our physical brains economize and selects just a few memorable moments for our hearts to meditate on. What you have for breakfast over the past fifty years is irrelevant to today's decisions. Remembering the highlights of your marriage and your childhood are important. Those memories can enrich our decision making. So our brains try to keep easy recall memories to seven or at most nine. If we want any more memories we have to consciously make a list and memorize a list, up to nine lists we can easily access. The problem with the lists is that we have to recall the list before we can recall the memory. It takes longer to remember the actual memory.

It's good for our minds to do this. It helps us know what is very good and very bad. It helps us make value judgments. Our minds treasure some things and put others further away from our heart, the center of our thinking. There are some persons who remember everything. These super savants hold dearly every crack in the road, every day of the week as much as any other. They recall what they were doing on September 11, 2001 as well as what they were doing on August 11, 2001.

Nine books.

There are some book I enjoyed reading, some I didn't. Yet there are nine books that I currently read over and over again. It's the books I'd want for my retirement on a deserted island. My current list includes *The Bible* and a collection of the best plays by William Shakespeare (Because I am not a participant of the Elizabethan age I rely upon scholars. I think the best single volume guide is Marjorie Gerber's *Shakespeare After All* 2004.). *The Chronicles of Narnia, Mere Christianity,* a book by writer Dallas Willard are my Christian digest this year.

I love big art and photography books. There's a certain point, late in twentieth century history, color reproduction comes close to capturing the colored beauty of art. By the twenty-first century the time had arrived. I love to read and stare at the pages of Marilyn Stockyard's *Art History* Revised Second Edition (2005). Yet there are a few paintings that you just have to see in person. A photographic reproduction doesn't do justice. I didn't realize that John Constable added depth to *Salisbury Cathedral from the Meadows* (1831) by adding extra layers of paint to the meadow grass. I saw it only after seeing the original at the National Gallery, London. It was extraordinary. I was seeing through Constable's eyes.

History books are very important for meditation. When you go to the hospital the staff writes up a medical history. When you buy a used car you want a crash and repair history. When you go on a date you should know the person's family and friendship history (Does your date's parents talk around a morning and evening cup of coffee, or scotch and soda under the table?). The future is in the past. This year I am reading again and again *From Dawn to Decadence: 500 Years of Western Culture* (2000) by Jacques Barzun. Other years I meditated fat books about American history, aviation and presidential biography.

In my youth and old age I love poetry. This year I'm reading and listening to *The Poets' Corner: The One-and-Only Poetry Book for the Whole Family* (2007) Compiled by John Lithgow. Read the book to your children. So much fun and wisdom.

886)
Nine pictures.

A photograph or a painting does matter to the heart. Excluding family photos, here's two of my favorites:

The choice of these two pictures and others is worthy of another book. I have already alluded to the the English artist John Constable. In his personal letters he writes about painting the glory of God in the common life of the English countryside. In his art he tries to show us how common people, livestock and the beauty of trees gives us glimpses of God's glory and light. John Sargent's *Carnation, Lily, Lily, Rose* (1886), perfectly fits the traditional idea of an art masterpiece. Art is skill and Sargent created his own method of displaying the Chinese lantern's luminosity. As a masterpiece presents an impressions of a moment in time. The creative placement of paint initiates a sense of pathos. Two girls surrounded by flowers in sunset skies, are like the twilight days of creation. The luminosity of the lanterns accords with our memories of late summer childhood memories. It's one of the paintings in the London Tate Gallery that receives the longest of gazes.

Nine Films

Some of us are lucky enough to find great films before wading through garbage. I pity professional film reviewers like Michael Medved who are paid to waist much time. Some days it may be one of America's dirtiest jobs. The very best cinema are like Jesus' parables. They make you think and see more than at first meets the eye. It's hard to have a collection of best films on permanent display in my neural gallery. Right now I include *It's a Wonderful Life* (1946), *Awakenings* (1990), *Shadowlands* (1993), and *Trip to Bountiful* (1985). Others are on temporary display.

A warning. There is much more violence in films as there are in city streets. The Jewish film director Fritz Lang gives a reasoned explanation. Earlier generations of Europeans and Americans accepted that God's Judgment Day was the biggest thing to fear. Yet today's world denies divine judgment. If there is no final judgment and eternal rewards then big guns, big bucks together rule society, not hope and justice. Some films with violence are anti-violent. John Ford's two films *The Searchers* (1956) and *The Man Who Shot Liberty Valance* (1962) preach two antidotes. In the former it is mercy, love and family; in the latter it is courage and the rule of law. Clint Eastwood's *Gran Torino* (2008) gives the grand Christian response: love of neighbor, martyrdom,. trust in God's mercy and a place in God's eternal home.

There are good and bad romance films. Many are ripe with folly. Despite the what our commercially saturated environment says, sex is not center of romance or marriage. Romance is finding a friend who will be there as a friend when you are old and gray and when you are not between the sheets. And this is where Americans are woefully misinformed. I never understood why the most alluring of women failed more often than the hometown beauty. They relied so much on the beauty that their conversations and character had become shallow, as shallow as their makeup. That's why I find a film like *Shadowlands* so emotionally honest and appealing.

Nine Pieces of Music

Get the Rolling Stone out of your head if you want "satisfaction." Music worth listening to does have a catchy melody but it also have layers of depth. I love Mendelssohn's *Violin Concerto in E Minor* and Bach's St. Matthew's Passion. There are some opera tunes that I love and at the same time feel indifferent to the opera itself. Rogers and Hammerstein's best works are romantic and can be listened to as worship of God. Christianity sings, "No other Love Have I." Expand your listening repertoire. Include classic, pop, ethnic, Broadway, and Jazz.

Avoid loud screeching guitars and heavy bass beat. Loud, rock music desensitizes our ears. They weaken hearing skills.

What are your nine melodies that you listen to over and again?

13 friends.

Thirteen friends, not nine. I remember reading somewhere that whenever you have more than thirteen in a group not all can participate. You will have then participants and audience. You will have friends and acquaintances.

Surprise! Jesus had an inner circle of twelve he called friends. Of course you will think of your spouse and your children. I think of my grand aunt Ruth. But who are the twelve outside your home? Do they lead you to happiness and virtue? Or chaos and a hangover?

One God

That's all you need. Choose wisely.

Appendix 2

Genesis 1: The Prologue of All Prologues

The tragedy of *Romeo and Juliet* begins with a fourteen line stage prologue spoken in verse. It sets the stage for the events that follow:

> Two households, both alike in dignity,
> In fair Verona, where we lay our scene,
> From ancient grudge break to new mutiny,
> Where civil blood makes civil hands unclean.
> From forth the fatal loins of these two foes
> A pair of star-cross'd lovers take their life;
> Whole misadventured piteous overthrows
> Do with their death bury their parents' strife.
> The fearful passage of their death-mark'd love,
> And the continuance of their parents' rage,
> Which, but their children's end, nought could remove,
> Is now the two hours' traffic of our stage;
> The which if you with patient ears attend,
> What here shall miss, our toil shall strive to mend.

The prologue tells us that the stage is the Italian city of Verona. It is really the stage of the Globe Theatre but the first speaker, "the chorus," tells us to see it differently. Shakespeare's prologue tells his audience to wait patiently and learn a lesson for their London days "Where civil blood makes civil hands unclean."

Musical plays and nearly all operas also have their prologues. Leonard Bernstein and Stephen Sondheim's *West Side Story* begins with a prologue of music and dance. Bongo drops and violins playing a discordant chord speaks to our minds that all is not well on the West Side of New York. The notes disagreeably resonate the strings of the heart and we desire a resolution. The choreography by Jerome Robbins is expressive of the tension and freedom of two rival gangs. It is a delight in the film, even better as a live performance (Though I have walked around the gang areas of Dorchester, Boston and Germantown, Philadelphia, I don't remember seeing any youth's dancing on their toes.).

Like many works of music and literature the prologue of *West Side Story* finds it ultimate resolution in an epilogue. The beginning has an end. Bernstein's epilogue is not a comedic. In a true comedy the couple gets married and live happily ever after. A tragedy ends in death. But like Shakespeare's *Romeo and Juliet*, the epilogue of *West Side Story* presents the audience the hope of redemption. Will their death's bring the wedding of two gangs into one heart? There is hope. For the Shakespearean audience the unanswered question is whether love can bring Protestant and Catholic England together. For Bernstein and Sondheim's Mid-twentieth century audience will different races and ethnicity merge "in America."

Prologues and epilogues have been a part of human culture since the beginning. Children and folk tales often begin the prologue with "Once upon a time . . ." If it's a happy tale story, conclude by saying, "and they lived happily ever after. The more well know prologues of Western Literature are found in the two works of Homer, Dante's *Divine Comedy,* Herman Melville's *Moby Dick,* Luke's Gospel and the Gospel of John. It is the latter prologue that echoes the first chapter of the entire Bible.

A prologue has the following elements:

1. Establishes the setting of the story
2. Gives essential details to the story
3. Provide information of any prior events.
4. Spoken in omniscient and often expresses the author's perspective.

And what of the Bible, the West's most widely read work of literature? Does it also have a prologue and an epilogue? No scholar doubts that *The Book of Job, Luke's Gospel and The Gospel of John* begins with a prologue.

John's prologue is of particular importance to the story of Genesis. It's content and style intentionally imitates Genesis One. But its message is not about science. It's about something far more important, life itself. If Jesus had been born in our time and John had a PhD in biophysics from MIT, would his education enabled him to describe the light of the world?

John wants us to understand that we are undergoing a new creation. The first Creation ends with man/Adam; the second begins with Christ, the new Adam.

John does not tell us anything about science, biology or ecosystems. His words are about something far greater. The message is about life and eternal life itself.

With developments of science in the eighteenth century, the industrial and Darwinian revolutions in the nineteenth, the American environment shifted away from the power of God to nature's god. Before, the Creator was honored as greater than machinations of creation. Baptist theologian Augustus H. Strong's *Systematic Theology* and the Presbyterian T*he Fundamentals* saw no contradiction between evolution, geology and the Bible. At the same time others began judging God by science. Both the fiery preaching of God's power and the high priests of industrial profits and intellectual vanity forsook the deep glory of the creation story. The former preached Genesis 1 as good science, the latter as bad and worthless.

End Notes

1. The late Penor Rinpoche defends his decision at http://www.sangyetashiling.dk/kt/seagal.htm

2. M. A. S. Abdel Haleem trans., *The Qur'an: A New Translation* (New York: Oxford University Press, 2004), p. 54.

3. The quote can be found on nearly every Winnie the Pooh website. Yet none site the book or page.

4. Charles Darwin, *The Descent of Man* (1871), p. 168

5. William Saroyan, *The Human Comedy* (New York: Harcourt, Brace and Company, 1943), p. 203f.

6. *Objective Knowledge: An Evolutionary Approach*, 1972. Popper, K.R. (1977), K.R. Popper and J.C. Eccles, *The Self and its Brain* (Berlin/Heidelberg/London/New York: Springer-Verlag, 1977).

7. Paul Vitz, "Analog Art and Digital Art: A Brain-Hemisphere Critique of Modern Painting" in *The Foundations of Aesthetics, Art & Art Education* Edited by Frank H. Farley and Ronald W. Neperud (New York: Praegar, 1988), p. 43-86.

8. Robert Dallek, *Flawed Giant: Lyndon Johnson and His Times 1961-1973* (New York: Oxford University Press, 1999) p. 4.

9. Robert Boyd Munger, *My Heart Christ's Home* (Downers Grove, IL: Inter Varsity Press, Expanded edition (1986).

10. http://www.post-trib.com/news/123108,PollackArt.article.

11. From W. Lehman, *Meister Eckhart*, Gottingen, 1917, p. 243, quoted in R. Otto, *The Idea of the Holy,* Oxford University Press, *1923,* p. 196.

For Further Reading

[This particular list is for those who wish to question or understand my luminist philosophy.

To enjoy 'seeing the unseen,' I recommend Pascal, Elizabeth Eliott, Dallas Willard, Phillip Yancy, C. S. Lewis, many, but not all Christian biographies. Don't waste your time reading books by people who claim a 'special anointing.' Some dancers can't walk a strait line when there off the stage.

Start a diary. Collect, recollect and write down what really brings joy.]

Bevington, David. Editor. *The Necessary Shakespeare*. New York: Longman, 2002.

Brodie, Thomas L. *Genesis as Dialogue: A Literary, Historical, & Theological*
Commentary. New York: Oxford University Press, 2001.

Duncan, Ken. *America Wide.* Wamberal, Australia: Ken Duncan Panographs, 2001.

Eccles, Sir John. Editor. *Mind and Brain: The Many-Faceted Problems.* New York: Paragon House, 1985.

Finney, Paul Corby. *The Invisible God: The Earliest Christians on Art.* New York: Oxford University Press, 1994.

Gombrich, E. H. *Art and Illusion: A Study in the Psychology of Pictorial Representation.* Sixth Edition. London: Phaidon Press, 2004.

Johnson, Paul. *Art: A New History.* New York: Harper Collins, 2003.

Nouwen, Henry J. M. *The Return of the Prodigal Son.* New York: Doubleday, 1992.

Robinson, Daniel N. *Consciousness and Mental Life.* New York: Columbia University Press, 2008.

Schaefer, Francis. *Art and the Bible.* Downers Grove, IL: InterVarsity Press, 1973.

Stokstad, Marilyn. *Art History.* Revised Second Edition. Upper Saddle River, NJ: Pearson Education, Inc., 2005

Dana Roberts has taught history and World Religions in colleges and universities. He has written a number of books and articles on China and Christianity in China. His research on art and religion has taken him to museums in Asia, The United States and England.

If you enjoyed reading this book. You will enjoy attending one of the author's Bible and Art audio-visual presentations:

The Genesis of Virtue and Beauty

The Changing Image of Chinese Art

John Constable, A Love Story

Seeing the Unseen in American Landscape

Renaissance Art, North and South

The Art of Seeing Face to Face

Healing the Image of God

*The Great Chain of Being
and Eating*

For further information contact; Dana Roberts at . . .

Hainan1@hotmail.com.